THE
BIVOCATIONAL
PASTOR

LUTHER M. DORR

BROADMAN PRESS
Nashville, Tennessee

ISBN: 0-8054-2604-3
Dewey Decimal Classification: 253
Subject Heading: BIVOCATIONAL PASTORS
Library of Congress Catalog Card Number: 87-27727

Printed in the United States of America

Unless otherwise indicated, Scripture quotations are from the King James Version of the Bible. Scripture quotations marked (GNB) are from the *Good News Bible,* the Bible in Today's English Version. Old Testament: Copyright © American Bible Society 1976; New Testament: Copyright © American Bible Society 1966, 1971, 1976. Used by permission.

Library of Congress Cataloging-in-Publication Data

Dorr, Luther M., 1932-
    The bivocational pastor.

    Bibliography: p.
    1. Clergy, Part-time. I. Title.
BV676.5D67   1988   253'.2   87-27727
ISBN 0-8054-2604-3

Preface

This book grew out of three basic concerns. The first is a consciousness that bivocationalism is a growing fact of life for more and more ministers today. The second is a commitment to the validity and legitimacy of bivocationalism as a needed form of ministry in the twentieth century. The third is a concern that those men serving today and in the future as bivocationals be given the recognition and encouragement they deserve.

The term *bivocational* has been used predominately throughout the book. The term refers to a minister who earns his living through two vocations. He normally works about 35-40 hours per week at the nonchurch vocation and about 25-30 hours per week with a church. The nonchurch vocation is usually a secular vocation, though in a few instances it might be a religious one but not in a local church.

Bivocational ministers have many similarities, regardless of their denomination. I am a Southern Baptist. I teach in a Southern Baptist seminary. We have about ten thousand bivocational ministers in our Convention. Other denominations also report large numbers of their ministers as having both secular and church vocations. More and more information is becoming available to encourage and help these ministers in their unique situation.

This book should be helpful to several groups of people. Prospective bivocational ministers and churches should find information and help in facing the possibilities of bivocationalism. Students in college, seminary, and in correspondence courses should find this book helpful. Denominations should find this book useful in informing their people of the history, nature, and potential for bivocational ministry.

I am indebted to many people who assisted in the preparation of this book. My colleagues and students have been co-laborers in research and assembling the materials. Many colleagues among the New Orleans Baptist Theological Seminary faculty are bivocational. They teach here and serve churches as interim pastors, ministers of music, ministers of education, and other specialized ministries, such as organist and youth worker. Some serve on an interim basis; others serve longer periods of time. Many students have been or are now bivocational. Many of them have shared their experiences with me.

Doctors Gary Farley and Dale Holloway of the Home Mission Board of the Southern Baptist Convention (SBC) have contributed much encouragement and assistance in locating Southern Baptist materials and making invaluable suggestions concerning the content. Dr. H. Karl Reko's Doctor of Ministry thesis on worker-priest ministries in the Lutheran Church-Missouri Synod was most helpful for information from his denomination. The CODE Project provided materials gathered from dual-role ministers in Presbyterian, American Baptist, Episcopal, and the United Church of Christ denominations. Dr. James L. Lowery, Jr., of the Episcopal Church has some valuable and informative information in his published works.

Finally, Dr. Landrum P. Leavell, II, president of the New Orleans Seminary, and Dr. Jerry Breazeale, director of the School of Christian Training at New Orleans Seminary, have supported and encouraged me from the beginning. With Dr. Leavell's approval, Dr. Breazeale added a course on the bivocational pastor to the curriculum of the School of Christian Training and asked me to teach it.

May God bless bivocational ministers, their families, and their churches. May He use this specialized form of ministry to His glory.

Contents

1

Analyzing Paul, the Bivocational Preacher

The apostle Paul was perhaps the greatest man in the early church. He was a great Christian, evangelist, missionary, church planter, theologian, and writer of some of the New Testament. He was also a bivocational preacher. Bivocationalism has no more an illustrious example than the apostle Paul, the tentmaker-preacher. He could well be called the "Father of Bivocationalism."

The New Testament specifically mentions Paul's labors as a tentmaker in three cities: Thessalonica, Corinth, and Ephesus. He probably supported himself and his co-laborers in other places also, but we know that Paul worked as a tentmaker while preaching the gospel in these three cities.

Why was Paul a tentmaker? While many reasons may be given, these five factors were significant.

First, every Jewish boy was required to learn a trade. Cox wrote, "It was their [Jews] rule that every young man . . . should also be taught some handicraft."[1] The Talmud said, "What is commanded of a father towards his son?—To circumcise him, to teach him the law, to teach him a trade."[2] Rabbi Judah said, "He that teacheth not his son a trade, doth the same as if he taught him to be a thief."[3] Paul was probably taught the trade of tentmaking, which he later practiced as a missionary preacher.

Second, rabbis often could not accept pay for their religious services. They were supposed to support themselves. To receive money for services was often cause for suspicion as to the authenticity of their religious calling. William Barclay wrote,

> Here we have a vivid light on the kind of life that Paul lived. Paul was a Rabbi, but according to Jewish practice, every Rabbi must have a trade. He must take no money for preaching and teaching and must make his living by his own work and his own efforts.[4]

I. Howard Marshall also observed, "Since rabbis were expected to perform their religious and legal functions without demanding a fee, it was necessary for them to have some other sources of income."[5] Therefore, Paul was familiar with a religious worker earning his own living. It was probably the accepted thing to do rather than the unusual thing to do.

Third, tentmaking was a practical occupation for Saul of Tarsus. George Redding observed, "It was as natural for a Cilician boy to learn to work with cilice [the name for the wool produced in Cilicia] as for a boy in the South to work with cotton or one in the Northwest to take up lumbering."[6] Barclay explained:

> Tarsus was in Cilicia; in that province there were herds of a certain kind of goat with a special kind of fleece. Out of that fleece a cloth called *celicum* was made which was much used for making tents and curtains and hangings. Doubtless Paul worked at that trade, although the word means more than a tent-maker; it means a leather-worker and Paul must have been a skilled craftsman.[7]

Paul practiced a trade that was based on the product which made his home province world famous. Tentmaking was an occupation that would find a market most anywhere. The people in Thessalonica, Corinth, and Ephesus needed the products of Paul's skilled hands.

Fourth, the Greeks had a different concept of manual labor and of preaching for money than the Hebrews did. The Greeks despised manual labor. William Barclay said that no free Greek would willingly work with his hands.[8] Some

Christians had adopted this philosophy and would not work (2 Thess. 3:10-12). Paul's practice of providing his own livelihood was a needed example to the early church.

The Greeks also had no problems with earning a living through public speaking. From the *Biblical Illustrator* we learn that "some of the best incomes in Greece were made by clever lecturers; Paul was resolved he should never be mistaken for one of them."[9] Therefore, in Corinth and elsewhere Paul refused to be paid by the Christians in order to avoid suspicion of his motivation for preaching (1 Cor. 9:14-15).

Fifth, the practice of the Jewish priests had turned many people against them. Barclay observed that the word *priest* was a bad word for many. Whereas the average Jewish family ate meat only once a week, the priests ate meat daily and suffered physically from so rich a diet. Barclay concluded that Paul refused church financial support so he would not be classified with institutionally supported religious workers and would hopefully escape any taint on his ministry of the gospel.[10]

These five factors form a backdrop against which we see Paul making tents for a living while he preached the gospel. He gave more specific reasons for earning his own living in his correspondence with several churches where he had been a bivocational pastor.

Paul in Thessalonica

Paul, Silas, and possibly Timothy went to Thessalonica from Philippi. Paul remained there at least three weeks, preaching in the synagogue and staying in Jason's house. Paul's decision to be bivocational seems to have been influenced by the problems of deceit, greed, the fear of being a financial burden, and idleness among some church members.

Paul wrote that he had three goals in mind in Thessalonica: that his message would be without error, that he himself as messenger would be without impurity, and that his motivation would be without deceit (1 Thess. 2:3). He had no ulterior motive for preaching, such as an underlying desire for money or fame. Rather, he preached because God had entrusted to him the gospel (1 Thess. 2:4), and he wanted to obey God in order to please Him.

Paul mentioned the problem of greed in 1 Thessalonians 2:5. The love of money was a constant problem in the lives of Christians. Paul counseled that the overseer or bishop was to be free from the love of money (1 Tim. 3:3). Deacons were not to be "greedy of filthy lucre" (1 Tim. 3:8). All Christians were warned that the "love of money is the root of all evil" (1 Tim. 6:10). Consequently Paul's support of himself kept anyone from believing he preached only for money.

Supporting himself and the missionary team relieved the Christians from financial responsibility. Paul, Silas, and Timothy worked at hard labor night and day "because we would not be chargeable unto any of you" (1 Thess. 2:9). This enabled them to preach the gospel in Thessalonica without having to receive financial remuneration. The local church did not have to feel and bear an impossible financial responsibility for Paul and the team.

Paul also addressed the problem of idleness in Thessalonica by being a tentmaker (2 Thess. 3:6-12). Some believers in the church wouldn't work (2 Thess. 3:10-11), but lived off the fruit of someone else's labor. Paul and his team believed that church support of God's ministers was a legitimate right, but they rejected this right in order to "make ourselves an ensample unto you to follow us" (2 Thess. 3:9). The model gave emphasis to the legitimacy and necessity of manual labor or earning one's own bread. Paul's example served to counter the Greek influence that manual labor was to be avoided.

Thus, Paul dealt with the problems of deceit, greed, financial burden, and idleness through bivocationalism. At the same time he won the lost, developed new Christians, and grew the church in the city of Thessalonica.

Church support was not ruled out completely. The Philippians sent Paul gifts several times while he was in Thessalonica (Phil. 4:15-16). But Paul chose to refuse financial support from the local believers. He earned most of his living himself. Tentmaking was possible for Paul because of his early boyhood training. Tentmaking was preferred by Paul because of the needs of the church. Tentmaking became the perfect solution for Paul, his associates, the believers in the new, small church, and the commission of God to carry the gospel to the city of Thessalonica.[11]

Paul in Corinth

Corinth is the second place Paul labored as a tentmaker. He served in that city at least one and one-half years (Acts 18:11). Sosthenes, Apollos, and Timothy may have been helpers or team members at Corinth.

Acts 18:1-4 gives us insight into how Paul might have operated in a city. Upon arriving in Corinth, he found Aquila and Priscilla who were also tentmakers. He lodged and labored with them in the business of making tents.

A. T. Robertson wrote, "Edersheim says that a Jewish guild always kept together."[12] Therefore, Paul found the guild of tentmakers upon his arrival in Corinth. This group gave him a place to stay and a work to do for financial support. Then he went to the synagogue and began his ministry of preaching the gospel.

A bivocational pastor today needs a secular skill that is portable and marketable. Tentmaking was such a skill for Paul. Tentmaking probably included many kinds of work. It has been suggested that tentmaking could mean:
1. Permanent tent homes for use by families.
2. Portable tents for use by soldiers or people who traveled long journeys.
3. Umbrellas for use in the caravans to provide protection from the sun.
4. Hangings or curtains for use in theaters.
5. Weavings of all sorts from the goat's hair or other materials.

Paul could do this kind of work on his own schedule with freedom to manage his time as he saw fit.

Paul probably found many evangelistic contacts through tentmaking. Every member of the guild was a contact for Christ. Each Jewish home became a mission field. The synagogue provided an opportunity to speak for the Lord. Each customer who purchased Paul's goods was a potential prospect. Gentiles were won to the Lord (Acts 18:6-7), and these converts opened up their homes and circles of friends to the gospel. Paul also planned door-to-door or house-to-house visitation in Ephesus (Acts 20:20). Tentmaking opened many doors in Corinth for the gospel.

Paul gave several reasons for having earned a living when he was in Corinth. He had not wanted to hinder the gospel (1 Cor. 8:12). He had not wanted to be suspected of preaching for money. Therefore, by working as a tentmaker, he had offered the gospel "without charge" (1 Cor. 8:13).

Paul had also wanted to demonstrate that Christians often have to give up their rights for the sake of harmony in the church and also for the sake of the effectiveness of the gospel. In the turmoil in the church caused by the question of whether to eat meat offered to idols, Paul counseled the Corinthians to guard against using their freedom in such a way as to cause others to stumble (1 Cor. 8:9). The principle he taught and practiced was the principle of becoming "all things to all men, that I might by all means save some" (1 Cor. 9:22).

A second reason Paul gave for self-support was that he had not wanted to be a burden to the church (2 Cor. 11:9). The Macedonian churches had supplied Paul's needs some of the time (1 Cor. 11:9). Evidently Paul's income came from tentmaking some of the time and from the gifts of the Macedonian Christians at other times. Some in the church at Corinth didn't like the fact that Paul had supported himself (2 Cor. 11:7). He said that he had refused support from them because he loved them (2 Cor. 11:11). He further indicated that should he return to Corinth he would follow the same practice of self-support because "I seek not yours, but you" (2 Cor. 12:14).

Paul ended his defense for self-support and for refusing local church support at Corinth with these famous words: "I will very gladly spend and be spent for you" (2 Cor. 12:15). Tentmaking was hard work. The word *labour* in 1 Corinthians 4:12 means "to labor to the point of weariness." Paul's income was not always adequate, for he said that "we both hunger, and thirst, and are naked" (1 Cor. 4:11). Yet, he had labored among them because he loved the Lord, the gospel, and the people of Corinth.

When the modern-day tentmaker gives all and is tempted to ask, "Is it worth it?" he can find no better answer then that of Paul: "I will very gladly spend and be spent for you" (2 Cor. 12:15).

Bivocationalism is not an excuse for a second-rate performance by a minister. What fully supported minister in this age or any age has made a greater contribution to theological understanding, to ethical insight, and to mission strategy than did Paul, the bivocational minister? He put his best into his calling. He is a worthy model for all of us in ministry.[13]

Paul at Ephesus

Paul's length of service in Ephesus was over three years (Acts 20:31). It was one of his longest tentures of service with one church about which we know. On the way to Jerusalem toward the last of his missionary journeys, Paul met with the elders of the church of Ephesus. While reviewing his ministry in Ephesus, he revealed that he had supported himself and those who labored with him (Acts 20:34). Paul offered two reasons or motivations for self-support: to help the weak and to experience the fact that giving is more blessed than receiving (Acts 20:35).

How did self-support enable Paul and the missionary team to help the weak? Possibly the weak people he had in mind were the struggling believers of the Ephesian church. Self-support relieved them of the financial burden of supporting a team of missionaries. Self-support enabled the Ephesians to have Paul and the team with them for three or more years.

Today bivocationalism enables some churches to have pastors who otherwise could not afford them if full financial support were required. Bivocationalism also enables churches to have ministers with qualifications the church could not afford if full-time support were expected from the church.

Paul's self-support might have helped the weak also by providing additional money for the church to use in mission outreach and ministry. A bivocational pastor's self-support often frees budget money in the church for use in other needy areas. Some bivocational pastors give more money to their churches through tithes and offerings than the churches pay them.

The second reason given by Paul for self-support was the truthfulness of the promise of Christ: "It is more blessed to give than to receive" (Acts 20:35). It is interesting that the only place this statement of Jesus occurs in the New Testament is in Paul's explanation of why he was bivocational in Ephesus.

Ministers need to be reminded of this truth about giving, and they need to practice it. Receiving a full-time salary from a church is legitimate and helpful. But supporting yourself in order to meet a need in a church or mission situation is a blessing all its own. Local church support might be the plan of God for most ministers. But God calls some ministers to support themselves in order to serve him in the work of the gospel. Paul was one of those called upon to support himself. Whereas God supports most ministers through the local churches, God supports a number of His ministers through their own secular skills. Both groups deeply believe that the Lord provides the support.

Paul probably received financial support from at least three sources. He earned it himself by making tents. Churches other than the one he was serving sent him love gifts from time to time. And some churches he was serving probably gave him some financial support. Yet, Paul believed that God supplied all of his needs (Phil. 4:19).

Paul had learned to trust God for life's necessities (Phil. 4:11-12). He gave two important lessons in these comments to the Philippians. First, though Paul trusted in the Lord for supplying the resources for life's needs and he depended upon the Lord for strength for daily living (Phil. 4:13), he still had times when he said that he was hungry and suffered need (Phil. 4:12). Did the Lord fail Paul? Evidently Paul saw no problem with a particular day or period of physical need and the underlying principle that God will provide. History doesn't teach us that Paul starved or froze to death. Therefore, the bivocational today who has to live one day at a time financially can take heart. Paul trusted God when he prospered; he trusted God when he was poor.

A second lesson has to do with the source of our financial expectations. Paul said, "My God shall supply" (v. 19). Didn't Paul work with his own hands for financial support? Didn't the Macedonian Christians send him financial support from time to time? Surely some local churches gave Paul money or food. Yet Paul beleived God was the source of financial expectations, whatever the human instrument or channel.

The bivocational minister doesn't believe that full-time church financial support is any more of God than personal financial self-support. The full-time pastor can't say "God supplies my needs" any more truthfully than the self-supporting pastor who also says, "God supplies my needs." Paul experienced both church support and self-support. He believed that God was the source of both. The self-supporting pastor trusts God for support as much as the full-time pastor does. God uses a secular skill as the means of support for one minister and the church budget as the means of support for another minister.[14]

These studies of Paul the tentmaker give bivocationalism today validity and inspiration. Paul's priorities were in order. He isn't remembered today as a great tentmaker but as a great minister of the gospel. He made tents in order to preach the gospel. His primary calling was to be a missionary to the Gentiles. To do so effectively he supported himself as a tentmaker.

Some ministers will be called of God to serve the gospel as bivocational pastors. They will serve Christ and witness for Him, supported by secular vocations. But, like Paul, their primary vocation will be that of preaching the gospel. Their secular vocations will pay the bills. William Carey once said, "My business is to witness for Christ. I make shoes just to pay my expenses."

Not all bivocationals feel alike about their two vocations. Some see the secular vocation supporting and making possible their religious vocation, as Paul seemed to view it. However, others believe that God has called them for ministry in their secular arena as much as in their religious setting. These ministers do not see tentmaking as "paying the bills" for their church work. Rather, both areas are important fields of ministry. Whatever view is held, all bivocationals need to be led of the Lord. They need to practice their bivocationalism as they understand the will of God for them. God calls all kinds of ministers for our needy world.

Notes

1. Samuel Cox, *An Expositor's Notebook* (Philadelphia: Smith, English, and Co., 1873), p. 424.

2. Ibid., p. 425.

3. A. T. Robertson, *The Acts of the Apostles,* Word Pictures in the New Testament, (Nashville: Broadman Press, 1930), 3:295.

4. William Barclay, *The Acts of the Apostles,* The Daily Study Bible, 2nd. ed. (Philadelphia: The Westminster Press, 1955), p. 147.

5. I. Howard Marshall, *The Acts of the Apostles,* The Tyndale New Testament *Commentaries,* R.V.G. Tasker, ed. (Grand Rapids: Wm. B. Eerdmans Publishing Company, 1981), p. 293.

6. George W. Redding, "Paul: Staking His Ministry in Tentmaking," *The Tentmaker's Journal,* July/August 1980, p. 3.

7. Barclay, p. 147.

8. William Barclay, *The Letter to the Corinthians*, The Daily Study Bible, 2nd ed. (Philadelphia: The Westminster Press, 1956), p. 85 *ff.*

9. Joseph S. Exell, ed. *I. Corinthians*, Biblical Illustrator (Grand Rapids: Baker Book House, n.d.), 17:533.

10. Barclay, *Corinthians*, pp. 89-90.

11. References forming the background for a study of Paul in Thessalonica are: Acts 17:1-9; 1 Thess. 2:3,5,9; 1 Thessalonians 4:11-12; 2 Thessalonians 3:7-9,12; and Philippians 4:16.

12. Robertson, p. 294.

13. References forming the background for a study of Paul in Corinth are: Acts 18:1-11; 1 Corinthians 4:10-13; 1 Corinthians 9; 2 Corinthians 11:7-9; 2 Corinthians 12:11-18.

14. References forming the background for a study of Paul in Ephesus are: Acts 19:1-41; Acts 20:33-35.

2

Reviewing the Past

The concept of a bivocational minister is not new. Bivocationalism has a rich heritage. This chapter surveys the biblical and historical background of the bivocational ministry.

Biblical Background

What do we find when we survey the Bible with reference to bivocationalism? Did all of God's ministers receive their livelihood from religious institutions? Did they support themselves?

OLD TESTAMENT

Dale Holloway is the national consultant for bivocational ministries in the Southern Baptist Convention. In a brochure entitled *Ministers of the Marketplace,* Holloway said that bivocationalism is an old concept. He mentioned Amos and Melchizedek as examples of Old Testament persons who had both secular and religious ministries. Amos was a farmer and a prophet. Melchizedek was a king and a priest.[1]

Pastoral support by religious institutions, such as the tabernacle, the Temple, or a local church, came in due time. But the early servants of God supported themselves. We would call Adam a farmer, for he was commanded to subdue the earth, to have dominion over its creatures, and to earn his living from the sweat of his brow (Gen. 1:28; Gen. 3:17-19). Abel was a shepherd, and Cain was a "tiller of the ground" (Gen. 4:2). Noah farmed (Gen. 9:1-2); Abraham raised cattle (Gen. 13:2). God supported all of these Old Testament servants through some secular means as they fulfilled their places in His plans for His people.

Moses was supported by the Egyptian court for forty years. He served as a shepherd for his father-in-law, Jethro, for the next forty years. Only in the last forty years of wilderness wandering did God supply Moses' livelihood directly. Once in Canaan, all the tribes, except the tribe of Levi (Josh. 13:14), earned their living from their land inheritance. Joshua eventually settled on his land and built Timnath (Josh. 19:50). Gideon, a judge, threshed wheat (Judg. 6:11). The norm through those early years seems to have been self-support rather than some form of institutional support.

When we come to the prophets, we see Amos as a clear example of a man with two vocations. He was a farmer/ prophet. Amos's own testimony was that he was a "herdsman, and a gatherer of sycomore fruit" (Amos 7:14). Hosea's father has been called "a middle-class merchant, perhaps a baker."[2] Hosea probably worked in the family business with him. Ezekiel and Jeremiah came from priestly families, which were probably supported to some degree by the Jerusalem Temple organization. Daniel came from a family of nobility, for he was deported to Babylon in the first group of Israel's best young men (Dan. 1:3-6). He was supported in Babylonian Exile by the Babylonian government.

Of course, no one can be dogmatic about these Old Testament ministers. The Levites seemed to have been supported by their function in the Temple. When a prophet served in the court of a particular king, he was probably supported by that king's government. However, the mainstream of prophets was predominately self-supporting or bivocational in their ministries to the nation of Israel.

J. Christy Wilson, Jr., proposed this same thesis. He wrote:

Many of the godly men and women in the Old Testament were self-supporting witnesses. . . . Adam was a cultivator, Abel was a sheep farmer, Abraham was a cattle raiser, Hagar was a domestic worker, Isaac was a farmer, Rebekah was a

water carrier, Jacob was a roving rancher, Rachel was a
sheep herder, Joseph was a premier, Miriam was a baby-
sitter, Moses was a flock-grazer, Bezaleel was a skilled ar-
tificer, Joshua was a military commander, Rahab was an inn-
keeper, Deborah was a national deliverer, Gideon was a
military leader, Samson was a champion fighter, Ruth was a
gleaner, Boaz was a grain grower, David was a ruler, the
Queen of Sheba was an administrator, Job was a gentleman
farmer, Amos was a sharecropper, Baruch was a writer, Daniel was a prime minister, Shadrach, Meshach, and Abednego
were provincial administrators, Queen Esther was a ruler,
and Nehemiah was a governor.[3]

The role of the Jewish scribes in the life of Israel from Ezra
to the New Testament sheds some light on self-support. The
scribes served as teachers of the law and as judges in religious matters in Israel. They were not allowed to accept
payment from those they taught or judged. The Mishna stated the following law: "If anyone accept pay for rendering
judgment, his judgment is null and void."[4] Consequently,
unless a scribe inherited wealth from his family, he had a
secular vocation while pursuing his ministry of the law.

By the time of the New Testament, all scribes evidently
did not follow this rule. Jesus warned the people of scribes
who "devour widows' houses" (Mark 12:40) and who are
greedy (Luke 16:14). These scribes were to be avoided. But
as a general principle, the scribes were "For the most part
students of the law who supported themselves by a trade,
declining to accept remuneration for their labours."[5] This
practice probably had an important influence on Paul's decision to refuse church support in various places where he
served.

NEW TESTAMENT

When we turn to the New Testament, we find the clearest
biblical testimony of bivocationalism in all of the Bible. That
testimony comes from the practice and teachings of Paul the
tentmaker. Paul's practice has influenced many ministers.

Pastor Michael E. Haynes expressed his call to the Twelfth Baptist Church of Roxbury, Massachusetts, as a bivocational pastor as being led to become a member of the apostle Paul's "fraternity of tentmakers."[6]

We also have glimpses into the practices of several people in the New Testament other than Paul. We do not have much insight into how Jesus and His disciples were supported. Luke said that certain women and "many others, . . . ministered unto him of their substance" (Luke 8:1-3). John referred to "the bag" containing money used for buying food and giving to the poor (John 13:29). How was the bag supplied? Could Jesus and the disciples have spent some of their time earning some of their income? Jesus was a carpenter, and several of the disciples were commercial fishermen.

Other names in the New Testament come to mind when we think of self-support. George Redding called Luke a "bivocational physician/evangelist."[7] The apostle Paul spoke of Zenas the lawyer (Titus 3:13). Barnabas probably supported himself when working alone as a missionary just as he supported himself when working in partnership with Paul (1 Cor. 9:6).

Christy Wilson also suggested this idea of self-support for people in the New Testament when he wrote:

> Also, in the New Testament our Lord's stepfather, Joseph, was a carpenter, Martha was a housekeeper, Zacchaeus was a tax collector, Nicodemus and Joseph of Arimathea were supreme-court councillors, Barnabas was a landowner, Cornelius was an officer, Luke was a doctor, Priscilla, Aquila, and Paul were tentmakers, Lydia was a purple-dye seller, Zenas was a lawyer, and Erastus was a city treasurer.[8]

Historical Background

When we leave the period covered by the New Testament, we find that bivocationalism was the norm for many ministers throughout the centuries to our present day. John Elliott wrote:

Dual Role or tentmaking ministry has been an approved and
effective part of the Christian church from the beginning. It
has served well to meet the needs of Paul at Philippi, the
monks in medieval cloisters, the Reformers adrift from tradi-
tional controls and financial stability, the pioneer families on
the frontier plains, or struggling congregations on the cross-
roads of twentieth-century America.[9]

100 - 600

Most clergymen in the first few centuries supported themselves. James Lowery also observed that the self-supporting
clergyman "is a historic form of ministry and was the norm
in the first three or four centuries of church history."[10] Richard Lenski, commenting on 1 Peter 5:2, said, "In our day
shameful gain generally consists in eagerness to get a large
salary . . . but we should remember that in apostolic times
elders were not salaried or paid."[11]

The testimony of research is almost universal that bivocationalism was the normal practice in the early church. Thurman Allred of the Southern Baptist Convention said: "The
advent of the full-time pastorate is a fairly new arrival. From
the early days of the first century church until the founding
days of our nation practically all ministers earned their
livelihood from a skilled vocation."[12]

Marvin J. Miller of the Mennonite Church stated that
Paul's example of tentmaking provided an example for early
church leaders. Miller reported some of the evidence he
found from this early period: Chrysostom (ca. 347-407) mentioned some rural clergymen as yoking the oxen and driving
the plow. Spyridon, a bishop of Cyprus, was also a shepherd.
Zeno, whose church in Gaza was quite large, was a linen
weaver. One named Dionysius was a presbyter/physician,
and one named Theodorus was a presbyter/silversmith.
Basil reported that his priests were working and earning
their daily bread.[13]

When a church provided a salary for those who preached
in the early church the legitimacy of the preachers was sus-

pect. An illustration of this is found in some of the problems the early church had with the false doctrines advocated by Montanus of Phrygia. He paid the preachers who preached Montanist doctrines. When Apollonmius of Rome sought to refute the Montanist heresy, the major proof that the men were not true preachers was that Montanus paid them.[14]

The *Didache* is usually dated in the second century. It included instructions to apostles: "When the apostle goeth forth, let him take nothing but bread, [to suffice] till he reach his lodging: if he ask money he is a false prophet."[15]

500 - 1500

The monastic orders were a powerful force for over a thousand years in the Christian church. Manual labor was the practice of these brothers. Benedict of Nursia (died in AD 543) gave this rule for the Benedictine order: "The brothers ought to be occupied in manual labour," and concluded that "they are truly monks if they live by the labours of their hands; as did also our fathers and the apostles."[16]

Francis of Assisi (ca. 1223) gave this rule for the Franciscans: "I strictly command all the brothers never to receive coin or money either directly or through an intermediary."[17] John Wycliffe (ca. 1350) instructed his followers, the Lollards, that "friars are bound to gain their livelihood by the labours of their hands, and not by begging."[18] Quaker ministers were taught in 1678: "Those who have received this holy and unspotted gift [to be an Evangelist or Pastor], as they have freely received, so are they freely to give, without hire or bargaining, far less to use it as a trade to get money by it."[19]

Many ministers in the mainstream of the church did receive their support from their churches during this period. But many ministers believed church support was not best and, therefore, refused it. These men supported themselves as they served the Lord in their various callings.

1500 - 1900

Let's look now at the Reformation and then early American church history. What can be found here concerning bivocationalism?

John Elliott contended that the Reformation produced a flourish of bivocational ministers. He wrote:

> The Reformation excluded many preachers and church leaders from the blessing of the church. The new churches were led by clergy outside of apostolic succession. Once again the Dual Role minister emerged out of the necessity to survive, because the new congregations did not have the resources to support full-time clergy, and some of the groups were "underground."[20]

Bivocationalism served these Protestant ministers until their churches could become strong enough for full-time support. Many churches never grew financially to this stage.

Even when churches might have been financially able to support their minister full-time, often they did not. Karl Reko's research into dual-role ministries led him to the practice often used by the Church of England for her ministers in Colonial America. Reko wrote: "In colonial America, ministers of the Church of England often maintained themselves via the parson's glebe, a piece of land set aside for the pastor's use."[21] Through farming the minister could support himself while serving as pastor of the local church.

Baptists and Methodists in particular owe a deep debt of gratitude to the farmer/preacher and the school teacher/ preacher of the seventeenth and eighteenth centuries. These men followed the people to the frontier and supported themselves in order to preach the gospel. Thurman Allred, quoting from Zane Mason's book *Frontiersmen of the Faith*, envisioned these Baptist preachers as follows:

> The Baptist preachers lived and worked exactly as did their flocks: their dwellings were little cabins with dirt floors and instead of bedsteads, skin-covered, poll bunks. They cleared

the ground, split rails, planted corn, and raised hogs on equal terms with their parishioners.[22]

They preached sermons, pastored churches, and performed weddings and funerals while earning their living in some secular vocation.

A ministry supported by the church was frowned upon by many frontier people. James E. Carter wrote of this prevailing attitude to a paid ministry: "Baptists in the colonial period had trouble separating a paid ministry from the state controlled and state subsidized ministry of established churches."[23] Therefore, many churches made no plans to support their ministers. Church support was a long time coming in many areas of the frontier. J. M. Carroll, a prominent person in Texas Baptist history, told of his preacher-father who served pastorates in Mississippi, Arkansas, and Texas. His father did not receive as much as one hundred dollars in his whole life from all his churches. He supported his twelve children and the eleven orphans whom he raised by farming and merchandising.[24]

Early frontier history in America is a history of bivocational preachers who built churches. Many famous Baptist frontier preachers were self-supporting ministers of the gospel. John Leland was also a shoemaker and a farmer. John Clarke was a physician and lawyer. William Screven farmed twenty-six hundred acres of land in South Carolina. Isaac Backus lived off a large inheritance left to him by his father. R. E. B. Baylor of Baylor University fame was a judge and a congressman. Isaac McCoy was a schoolteacher, a weaver, a surveyor, and a farmer.[25]

This historical review indicates that bivocationalism isn't a new idea. In our day we tend to picture the minister as a religious professional, academically and professionally trained and serving a church which adequately supports him financially. A minister who doesn't fit this category tends to be somewhat suspect. We may think of him as a kind of second-class citizen. However, history reveals that through the years God has led His church and extended His work through godly persons who had to support themselves financially in order to serve Him. These roots are strong and deep. They will support any movement God has in mind today to do some of His work through bivocational ministers.

Notes

1. A brochure published by the Rural-Urban Missions Department of the Home Mission Board (HMB) of the Southern Baptist Convention, Atlanta, Georgia.

2. Merrill C. Tenney, ed., "Hosea," *The Zondervan Pictorial Bible Directory*, 3rd ed. (Grand Rapids, Zondervan Publishing House, 1964), p. 362.

3. J. Christy Wilson, Jr., *Today's Tentmakers* (Wheaton, Ill.: Tyndale House Publishers, 1981), p. 20.

4. James Orr, ed., "Scribes," *International Standard Bible Encyclopedia* (Grand Rapids: Wm. B. Eerdmans Publishers, 1960), 4:2705.

5. James Hastings, ed., "Scribes," *Enclyclopedia of Religion and Ethics*, (New York: Charles Scribner's Sons, 1920), 11:273.

6. Ronald J. Sider, ed., *Living More Simply: Biblical Principles and Practical Models* (Downers Grove, Ill.: Inter-Varsity Press, 1980), p. 139.

7. George Redding, "Paul: Staking His Ministry in Tentmaking," *The Tentmaker's Journal* (July-August 1980): 3.

8. Wilson, p. 21.

9. John Y. Elliott, *Our Pastor Has an Outside Job* (Valley Forge, Penn.: Judson Press, 1980), p. 20.

10. James L. Lowery, Jr., ed., *Case Histories of Tentmakers* (Wilton, Conn.: Morehouse-Barlow Co., 1976), p. v.

11. Richard C. H. Lenski, *Interpretation of Peter, John, Jude*, Vol. 11 (Minneapolis, Minn.: Augsburg Publishing House, 1966).

12. Thurman Allred, "Bi-Vocational: A Rich Heritage," *Church Administration* (November 1980): 39.

13. See Marvin J. Miller, *The Case for a Tentmaking Ministry* (Elkhart, Ind.: Mennonite Board of Missions, 1978), p. 3.

14. Eusebius, *Ecclesiastical History,* trans. by Christian Frederick Cruse (New York: Stanford & Swords, 1850), p. 201.

15. Henry Bettenson, ed., *Documents of the Christian Church,* 2nd ed. (London: Oxford University, 1975), p. 65.

16. Ibid., p. 123.

17. Ibid., p. 130.

18. Ibid., p. 174.

19. Ibid., p. 255.

20. Elliott, p. 18.

21. H. Karl Reko, "Determinative Factors in the Ability of Christ Seminary—Seminex Graduates to Conduct Worker-Priest Ministries in the United States." An unpublished D.Min. thesis of the Eden Theological Seminary, St. Louis, Mo., 1980, p. 22.

22. Allred, p. 39.

23. James E. Carter, "The Socioeconomic Status of Baptist Ministers in Historical Perspective," *Baptist History and Heritage* 15 (January 1980): 39.

24. Ibid.

25. See such books as O. K. and Marjorie Armstrong, *Baptists Who Shaped a Nation* (Nashville: Baptist Press, 1975); Frank T. Hoadley and Benjamin Browne, *Baptists Who Dared* (Valley Forge: Judson Press, 1980); and Mary Colson, *Heroes of the Faith* (Nashville: Baptist Press, 1954).

3

Surveying the Present

Bivocationalism is an important emphasis today in a number of denominations across our country. National church leaders are giving attention through conferences, materials, publicity, and encouragement to those who are already bivocational. Seminaries are offering special seminars and regular curriculum courses on the subject. Graduate students are doing research and working with projects in this area. This old concept is in vogue again today. Why has it reemerged and how prevalent is it among various denominations?

Why Has Bivocationalism Reemerged?

Bivocationalism has become an emphasis today for at least three reasons. These reasons are economic constraint, evangelism needs, and personal performance/call fulfillment.

Economic Constraint

One reason some ministers have become bivocational is economic. This by no means is the only reason, and it might not be the primary reason. But it is one of the reasons some churches and ministers have become bivocational.

James Lowery wrote about this dilemma faced by churches. He said, "The size of the local congregation that is the norm is below the level at which there can be a properly supported, ordained, professional staff, and a properly equipped church, parish house, and rectory/parsonage."[1] Therefore, churches are either folding up, combining with

other churches to share the same minister, receiving denominational supplement, or considering bivocational ministers
as the answer to this need.

Denominations do not agree on how many regularly attending persons are necessary for a church to be able to
afford a full-time pastor. John Elliott, a bivocational minister
from an American Baptist church reported that in 1950 the
number was 60. In 1980 that number had grown to 150. In
other words, Elliott believed that a minimum of 150 had to
attend a church each Sunday in order for that church to be
strong enough to support a full-time pastor.[2] The majority of
the churches in the USA fall below this figure.

Approximately half of all Southern Baptist churches have
about 240 members in their churches. A recent per capita
giving ratio in this Convention was about $250 person. That
would mean an income of about $60,000 for the church per
year. Thus, about 18,000 churches have an income of less
than $60,000 per year. Is a church able to maintain its proper-
ty, administer its programs, give to missions and other
needs, and also support its pastor adequately on this amount
of income and less?

A 1984 study of 7,034 small, rural, bivocational Southern
Baptist churches with memberships of 300 or less revealed
that the average total receipts in these churches per year
was $19,607 compared to $36,235 in 10,987 churches of the
same size with nonbivocational pastors.[3] For whatever reasons, some small churches have small incomes and cannot
support a minister full-time.

The situation is not getting better. Inflation increases faster than the average growth of giving in many churches.
Therefore, each year more and more churches are becoming
unable to support a pastor full-time. Many of these are turning to bivocationalism as the answer.

EVANGELISM OPPORTUNITIES

A second reason bivocationalism has reemerged is the opportunities it has for evangelism. Lost people need to be reached, and new missions and churches need to be established. Dr. William Tanner, past president of the Home Mission Board, SBC, recently said concerning bivocationalism: "We cannot wait for financial resources to start the thousands of new churches that need to be started. I think that's the reason God is calling out people to be bi-vocational ministers."[4] Dr. Grady C. Cothen, past president of The Sunday School Board, SBC, said, "We need a new emphasis on bivocational workers, especially in establishing new work."[5]

In recent history the church has tried different methods to reach lost people with the gospel of Christ. During World War II French Catholics initiated what they called the "Worker Priest Movement." Karl Reko called this movement "The French Experiment" and concluded that "there is no other instance of worker-priest ministry where the model was so consciously selected as a means of mission."[6] The ministers involved in this movement were like the bivocational pastors of today in that they earned their livelihood from a secular occupation. But these worker-priests also ministered totally in the secular arena.

The movement originated like this. Before the end of World War II, German armies carried almost a million French people to Germany to work in factories. The Catholic Church of France wanted to send priests with the workers to minister to them. When denied the right to do so by the German government, the Catholic Church authorized twenty-five clergymen to be conscripted by the Germans and sent to Germany as clandestine priests. Many of these were discovered and were arrested; many eventually died in concentration camps. Some survived, however, and reported their ministries to the church. Their ministries encouraged the church to promote worker-priest ministries after the war.[7] Although the numbers and interest have fluctuated from time to time, the worker-priests have continued to be a viable form of ministry by some denominations today.

Some Christians in England tried a similar movement in the 1950s. This movement was a mission effort to reach people who were difficult to reach by the organized church. Anne Grubb was one of these worker-priests.[8] Her group of worker-priests included a worker-deacon who was a packer in a factory, a priest who was an electrician's mate, another priest who was a factory worker who also served a parish church, another priest who was an engineer in a factory who also helped out in a local church while conducting services in his home, and still another who worked in a steel mill. All were trained in theological education and voluntarily chose the worker-priest approach for ministry.

One member of the group was asked if he thought such a highly trained theological person was wasting his time and training working full-time in a factory. He replied, "There are 13,000 heathen in this factory, and if that isn't enough for one man, I don't know what is."[9]

Anne Grubbs gave two compelling reasons for choosing the worker-priest approach to ministry. She wrote:

1. We believe that if we seriously intend to get over the Gospel to the people of our time, we must live it in the materialistic terms of money and work which they most easily understand. For our part, this means that we must express our faith by sharing fully the life of the working class. In our opinion, only on the basis of such a life is the preaching of the word likely to carry much conviction in modern industrial society.
2. We wish to proclaim the Gospel visibly "free of charge" (I Cor. IX:10). This point of view was expounded by St. Paul, and we often wonder why some people think it so revolutionary!"[10]

When asked if laypersons couldn't do this kind of work better, the group replied that they "felt an unanswerable call to the work" and that "certain developments in our work are only conceivable if they are led by an ordained man."[11]

Bivocationalism among Southern Baptists is as old as the Convention, which was organized in 1845. From the beginning of the Convention, some Baptist preachers have earned part of their income from a secular source and also served a church. Researchers have estimated that as late at the mid-1940s over 50 percent of all Southern Baptist preachers were bivocational. Full-time church support is a fairly recent development.

Following World War II Southern Baptists promoted bivocationalism as one strategy for missions. This strategy was known as the Tentmaker program. The Tentmaker program began in California in the early 1950s under the leadership of Home Missionary E. J. Combs and the Reverend Fred A. McCaulley, also of the Home Mission Board. College students wanted to work during the spring and summer at secular jobs in California to earn school money. They also wanted to do mission work at the same time. In 1951 Missionary Combs helped fifteen students find employment in the redwood timber of Northern California while working with him in churches and in mission outreach. These fifteen students started thirteen missions that summer.[12]

The following summer, sixty students went to California in the Tentmaker program. McCaulley was named director of the Southern Baptist Tentmaker Movement and asked to promote the tentmaker approach across the Southern Baptist Convention. The movement spread to other states. People other than students began volunteering to seek secular employment while working in mission opportunities. Many mission churches were started by bivocationals in many states.

CALL AND FULFILLMENT

A third factor in the growth of bivocational ministers has to do with a call from God to give one's ministry to a bivocational ministry. Many are finding fulfillment in this special kind of ministry. As more ministers and churches share their experiences, other ministers hear and consider it for themselves. People today are hearing about bivocationalism. Articles in denominational papers tell about successful bivocational men. Seminars and other training events are being planned with the bivocational person in mind. Some college and seminary students are being counseled to consider this form of ministry. As churches and denominations recognize the legitimacy and need for bivocational ministers, they will promote the idea and the needs will be more widely known. Consequently more ministers will consider it and will feel called to serve in a dual-role situation.

How Prevalent Is Bivocationalism?

SURVEY OF SELECTED DENOMINATIONS

Bivocationalism as a legitimate, alternative style of ministry has been the object of much study and experimentation in the last fifteen years. One such experimental project was conducted in 1975-1978 in western New York. Four denominations (United Presbyterian Church in the USA, American Baptist Convention, Protestant Episcopal Church, and the United Church of Christ) participated in a project later named CODE (Clergy Occupational Development and Employment) Project. The project had the following purposes:

> To assist interested clergy in exploring and becoming Dual-Role and to aid them in a legitimate alternative form of ministry which would be recognized by the denominations; to evaluate their ministries; and to make this information and the processes developed available to others throughout the church.[13]

Several conclusions came from this project. The participants discovered that clergymen could, indeed, serve the church, their congregations, their families, and their secular jobs effectively. The report concluded, "For some churches and some clergy, D-R [Dual-Role] is an effective alternative which is working."[14]

The CODE Project surveyed an area that included Rochester and Buffalo, New York, to determine the number of clergy involved in bivocational ministries. They found that about 10 percent of the churches had some form of bivocational ministry and that the number was growing each year.

The CODE Project also found that ministers wanted to go into dual-role situations for various reasons. One man served a church of eleven hundred members and was fully supported by the church. Yet he preferred a small church where more direct ministry and relationships could be experienced. He found a job with a social agency first and later in business customer relations. This pastor's denomination helped him find a small church which had been struggling financially to give minimum support to a full-time pastor. After a year's service with that church on a trial basis, the church called him as pastor. He gave the church twenty to twenty-four hours per week. They paid him accordingly. He agreed to serve the church in such areas as worship leadership, preaching, visitation of the sick and shut-ins, leading in church education, and seeking new members for the church. The church furnished him a home plus a salary, pension, travel expenses, and paid his utilities.

Another minister in the CODE Project had been in the ministry a year as an assistant pastor. This man's wife worked full-time. They had no children. They decided to move to another city and for him to become an assistant pastor in a church served by a bivocational pastor. The man and his wife relocated, and he found work as an engineer. The pastor and assistant pastor shared the preaching responsibilities in the church. The assistant pastor was given the responsibility of working with the young working couples in the church. He agreed to give twenty hours to the church. After a trial period of three months, the church called him as an assistant pastor. He purchased his own home. Both of these men served the church in a multiple staff relationship as bivocational ministers.

Denominations report growing numbers of bivocational

ministers. John Elliott reported, "Fifteen percent of all Episcopal priests nationally are self-supporting."[15] James Lowery
reported the figure somewhat higher when he wrote, "In the
Episcopal Church alone, 1,300 to 2,000 of the active Episcopal clergy in the United States (out of a total active number
of more than 9000), receive over half their total compensation from secular sources."[16] The differences could be due to
the different definitions of bivocationalism or different survey dates.

Other denominations also report growing numbers of
bivocational church leaders. Reko found that 7.2 percent of
all active United Church of Christ ministers were engaged in
secular occupations also.[17] Dr. Emmanuel McCall of the
Southern Baptist Home Mission Board estimated that at
least 70 percent of the pastors of Black National Baptist
churches are bivocational.[18] A survey taken in Louisville,
Kentucky, revealed that in the mid-1970s 83 percent of the
Black pastors were bivocational.[19] Churches where a language other than English is used tend to have bivocational
pastors due to their size and financial strength. Oscar Romo
of the Language Missions Department of the Southern Baptist Home Mission Board surveyed the Baptist Hispanic pastors in the Los Angeles area in the mid-1970s. He found that
all of them at that time were bivocational.[20] He also said that
from 75 to 85 percent of the Baptist Korean work was bivocational and that much of the Vietnamese work fell into this
same category.[21]

Overall, the number of ministers in bivocationalism continues to grow. Lyle Schaller was quoted as predicting that
one half of all ministers in the United States would be bivocational by the end of 1985.[22] J. T. Burdine quoted *Money*
magazine as saying, "Nearly half of the 365,000 Christian
ministers in the United States has a second occupation."[23]

THE SOUTHERN BAPTIST CONVENTION

Southern Baptists are giving serious attention to bivocationalism today. In 1976, 1980, and 1983 each church in the

Southern Baptist Convention was asked to report bivocational information on its annual Uniform Church Letter. That
information has been compiled by the Research Services
Department of The Sunday School Board of the SBC and
presented by the Southern Baptist Home Mission Board.[24]
Bivocationalism is an integral part of the life of Southern
Baptists.

To illustrate this fact, the numbers of bivocational pastors
in relationship to the total number of churches for each of the
three years are as follows:

Year	Bivocational Pastors	Total Churches
1976	9,415	35,073
1980	9,845	35,831
1983	9,026	36,531

These figures indicate a 4.6 percent increase between
1976-1980 and a 8.3 percent decrease between 1980-1983
among bivocational pastors in the Southern Baptist Convention. The total number of bivocationals could be higher because several hundred small churches usually do not report
each year. Many of these could have self-employed pastors.
Also, some mission churches that could have self-employed
pastors do not report separately from sponsoring churches.
These surveys do not reflect the number of bivocational
pastors who did not have pulpits at the time the churches
reported on their work. The number indicates only active
pastors with churches.

A downward trend in the total number of bivocationals in
the SBC is indicated in this information. The trend was up
in 1980 and down in 1983. Though the numbers show a decrease in total dual-role pastors in 1983, no projection was
made by the researchers that this trend would continue or
change. Bivocationalism will continue to receive recognition
and publicity as a needed ministry in the Convention.

The 1983 report revealed that bivocational pastors are
concentrated in the central part of the nation, in an area
which has boundaries including North Carolina, Kentucky,
Illinois, Missouri, Oklahoma, Texas, and all states South.

Alabama had 1,065 bivocational pastors in 1983, the largest number of any state convention. Tennessee had second with 941, and Texas had 931. Georgia had 872, and North Carolina 668.

The percentages of total churches with bivocational pastors in the state were as follows: Alabama had 35.1 percent; Tennessee, 33.7 percent; Illinois, 32.9 percent; Missouri, 31.9 percent; and Georgia, 29.2 percent.

The size of the churches having bivocational ministers was also found. In 1983, churches with less than 300 members had bivocational pastors in 90.0 percent of the cases. Almost 74.0 percent of all SBC churches with bivocational pastors had less than 200 members. In churches with memberships of 300 to 399, 5.5 percent had bivocationals. The percentage was 2.1 percent in churches of 400-499 membership. In churches with over 500 in membership, the percentage of bivocational pastors was 2.2 percent.

Where were these bivocational churches of the SBC located? The largest proportion, 71.7 percent in 1983, were in open country and villages. Some 13.3 percent were in towns and small cities (population 500-9,999). Medium cities (population 10,000-49,999) had 7.1 percent and large cities (population 50,000-up) had 7.9 percent.

Almost one out of every four SBC churches is served by a bivocational pastor. This fact will challenge Southern Baptists to give adequate recognition and support to these pastors. Southern Baptists see bivocationalism as a viable solution to the problem of adequate financial support for pastors of small churches. The bivocational pastor can also play a significant role in denominational expansion in the future.

THE CURRENT EMPHASIS TODAY

Church leaders are reacting to this current emphasis in various ways. Some call it the answer to the problems of the present and the hopes of the future. Others call it a perverted form of true ministry and a step backward from the best

Many are in between, recognizing it as an historical fact of the past, a reality in many places in the present, a probability for more and more ministers in the future, but at best only a necessary nuisance to be avoided if at all possible.

Because economic reasons are thrusting many ministers into bivocationalism, they are asking for genuine acceptance as true ministers. Many desire help and support from the religious community and denominational hierarchy. Therefore, bivocationalism is receiving attention in the form of recognition, encouragement, and help. Karl Reko did a survey of several denominational groups and their involvement in worker-priest or bivocational ministries. He reported a growing amount of interest in this form of ministry.[25]

For example, the Episcopal Church has given serious attention to its worker-priest ministers and to the possibilities of this form of ministry for the future. James L. Lowery, Jr., of the Episcopal Church has written widely in this area.[26] He advocates bivocationalism as one helpful solution to some of the problems facing the ministry in his denominations today.

Reko referred to discussions in the American Baptist Convention about how bivocationalism relates to that convention. The Presbyterian Church in the United States works through each of its presbyteries to determine relationships to worker-priests in its area. The United Presbyterian Church in 1974 asked that self-supporting ministries be seriously considered as real alternatives in ministry.

The Lutheran Church in America has recently studied ways of implementing the worker-priest ministries. Such matters as finances, ordination, and relationships have been the objects of much study and discussion. The United Church of Christ held an important worker-priest conference in 1971 to report on and explore the possibilities for this kind of ministry. The United Church of Christ reported 7.2 percent of all active UCC ministers were bivocational in 1973.[27]

Southern Baptists are placing a strong emphasis today on bivocational ministry. The Home Mission Board has a national consultant who promotes bivocationalism across the Convention. Many state conventions in the deep South conduct regular bivocational conferences for their bivocational ministers. These conferences are designed for fellowship, support, and encouragement. Several Southern Baptist seminaries offer either special courses or regular courses in the work of the bivocational pastor. National conferences on bivocationalism have been conducted at the Glorieta and Ridgecrest conference centers. Southern Baptists want to recognize and encourage the ten thousand active bivocationals. They also want to offer this form of ministry as a way to start new churches and reach unreached people.

In summary, bivocationalism is a movement that resurfaced in the last half of the twentieth century. For many ministers it is an economic necessity. For some it is a conscious choice as a way to meet needs that are out of the scope of church-supported ministers. Not all churches or ministers are interested in it, but many are. And many churches and ministers are finding fulfillment and effectiveness in working together in a bivocational relationship.

Notes

1. James L. Lowery, Jr., *Peers, Tents, and Owls* (New York: Morehouse-Barlow Co., 1973), p. 96.

2. John Y. Elliott, *Our Pastor Has an Outside Job* (Valley Forge, Penn.: Judson Press, 1980), p. 6.

3. Jack L. Washington, "Study of Bivocational Pastors and Churches in the Southern Baptist Convention, 1983" (Atlanta: Home Mission Board, SBC, 1984).

4. William G. Tanner, "Tanner Speaks His Mind on Bivocational Ministers," *The Tentmaker's Journal* (Fall 1981): 3.

5. Jim Lowry, Jr., "Reaching People Effort Launched," *Facts & Trends* (February 1982):4.

6. H. Karl Reko, "Determinative Factors in the Ability of Christ Seminary—Seminex Graduates to Conduct Worker-Priest Minis-

tries in the United States." An unpublished D.Min. thesis of the Eden Theological Seminary, St. Louis, Mo., 1980, p.40.

7. Ibid., p. 43 *ff.*

8. Anne Grubb, "English Worker Priests," *Frontier* (Winter 1960): 267 *ff.*

9. Ibid., p. 269.

10. Ibid., p. 267.

11. Ibid., p. 269.

12. See "Southern Baptist Tentmaker Tracks," 24 July 1956. A newsletter published by the SBC Home Mission Board, Atlanta, Ga.

13. Clergy Occupational Development and Employment Project, *Dual-Role Pastorates* (Rochester: Clergy Occupational and Employment Project, 1978), p. i. Referred to as CODE.

14. CODE, p. 6.

15. Elliott, p. 19.

16. James L. Lowery, Jr., ed., *Case Histories of Tent-Makers* (Wilton, Conn.: Morehouse-Barlow Co., 1976), p. 97.

17. Reko, p. 70.

18. Judy Touchton, "The Bi-vocational Pastor," *Home Missions* (October 1977):6.

19. Ibid.

20. Ibid.

21. Ibid.

22. Ibid., p. 5.

23. J. T. Burdine, "Adventure in Ministry—Bivocational Pastorates," *Church Administration* (January 1980):39.

24. See Washington.

25. Reko, p. 66 *ff.*

26. See Bibliography for materials by Lowery.

27. Reko, p. 70.

4

Viewing the Practices

What is bivocationalism? What kind of minister is a bivocational minister? How is his ministry different from other ministries? How is his ministry like any other ministry? What are the unique problems, possibilities, and needs of the minister who earns his income from both a secular source and a church?

Maybe you should meet some of these dual-role or bivocational servants of God. View their work through their eyes. Hear them share the problems and the advantages that they are finding in bivocational ministry. Their stories will probably remind you of one of the greatest bivocational preachers the church has ever had, the apostle Paul, the tentmaker.

In this chapter we will examine several bivocational pastors who are serving today.[1] Their stories are representative of many bivocational ministers. These stories include bivocational ministries being practiced today other than that of a pastor.

Ronny Robinson: Investigator and Preacher

Ronny Robinson, age thirty-eight and a native of Brookhaven, Mississippi, serves as pastor of the Mount Moriah Baptist Church near Brookhaven. He also serves forty to forty-five hours per week as an investigator in the Mississippi Department of Corrections. Ronny is bivocational because he feels called of God into this particular form of ministry. He has this conviction about his calling: "I don't feel that the bivocational pastor is a second-rate preacher who cannot support himself and his family by pastoring."

When asked to share the advantages he has found as a bivocational, he listed these:

1. The church members learn to be ministers.
2. The church has a greater spirit of cooperation.
3. The church has more money for real ministry.
4. The pastor has daily contact with the "outside world."
5. The church developes a "working family" spirit. All members try to do their part of the work.
6. Sermon materials comes from daily experiences.

Ronny also shared four disadvantages he struggles with most of the time.

1. Time: He must budget his time carefully.
2. Family: Ronny's family is the area that often gets cut short of attention.
3. Church Crises: He is not always available for every crisis on the church field. He has to follow up on it when he can.
4. Work: He must love to work with little time for fellowship and recreation.

How does Ronny try to put all of this together, keep everyone reasonably happy, and find meaning and fulfillment? He feels fortunate that the Department of Corrections seems to favor employing ministers. He has some freedom in the planning of his days. His superiors understand the responsibilities of a minister and are helpful in allowing him to work out his schedule.

There is no typical day for this investigator/pastor. Upon arriving at the courthouse office each morning, he plans his day. He often plans hospital or nursing home visits when his secular field work takes him near one of those facilities. He can schedule a counseling session now and then in his office if the person can come by the courthouse. He says, "I try to be a pastor first and an investigator second. I make my visits and contacts within the daily structure of my secular work." Ronny can do this because he lives near his work and near his church. His people also live in the same geographical area where much of his investigative work is done.

Family time begins as many days as is possible at 5:00 PM when he gets off from his secular job. The family shares the evening meal together. Often the television is then turned off, and some special time is spent together. Every other month Ronny and his family or just he and his wife take one or two days off. "These become special times when we try to get away and 're-group.'"

The Mount Moriah Baptist Church has an average Sunday morning attendance of around 150. Ronny also serves as the associational Church Training director in the Lincoln Baptist Association. He wishes for more time to serve outside his own church.

God has given the Reverend Ronny Robinson a vision for bivocationalism. He believes that smaller churches are not able to give much to missions if their budgets must support a full-time man and provide him a home. If such a large percentage of the budget didn't have to be used for pastoral salaries, more of it could be given to missions. Ronny says, "I feel that the bivocational pastor is an answer to God's challenge to win this world."

Ronny also wants to see the challenge of bivocationalism presented to young men in their early college years. He says, "If a man can feel God's call at this stage, then he can plan a career in a field where his professionalism will allow him to be his own boss." He warns that the frustrated bivocational men he knows are those who seem to be tied to a clock and have no control over their day's schedule.

A bivocational staff is a goal in Pastor Robinson's plans for his church. He says, "I find that I need staff help, but I have also found that bivocational staff members are my greatest asset. I have a bivocational minister of music, and we are looking for a bivocational youth director."

Jonah Parker: Orchardist and Pastor

Pastor Jonah Parker serves the Friendship Baptist Church, in rural Surry County, North Carolina. He is also a self-employed orchardist who grows apples in the Brush Mountains near Moravian Falls, North Carolina. The Friendship Baptist Church, located thirty-three miles from Parker's home and apple orchards, has a resident membership of 151 members.

Jonah Parker believes he is serving where he is because of the leadership of the Holy Spirit. Parker was called to preach when he was in his middle forties. He has served as he has been able to understand God's leadership. He says, "I do not like to be called a part-time preacher. I am just as much a preacher when I am on my John Deere tractor as a full-time preacher is on a golf cart. We all have to release the pressure somewhere."

As an apple grower, Jonah's secular work is seasonal. The hours per week spent in the orchards might vary from twenty to sixty, depending on the season. He has an apartment near the church where he and his wife live on the weekends. He still averages driving four hundred miles a week performing pastoral duties. Pastor Parker has this practice: "As for pastoring the church, when my people need me I drop everything and go. I am available every hour of every day, and my people know that." He also finds time to attend most of the associational and state Baptist meetings.

Jonah feels that the main advantage of being bivocational is being financially independent. He doesn't have to have income from his church to live. He also finds that the physical labor of his orchards serve the same purpose for him as golf, fishing, or any other hobby does for other preachers.

One disadvantage Jonah finds in bivocationalism is a feeling at times that he is trying to serve two masters. Apples need to be sprayed and sermons needs to be prepared at the same time. Parker admits to preaching a "Saturday night special" (sermons prepared on Saturday night before Sun-

day morning services) now and then following an exception-
ally busy week during harvest season. But he seeks to keep
his priorities in line by making the time to study even at the
expense of his apples. He exclaims, "It is difficult to find time
to study; bivocational pastors certainly don't watch much
television."

Jonah and his wife find time to be together. Their children
are grown and on their own, so she is by his side most of the
time. He likes part of this arrangement: His wife doesn't
have to hold a public job to help support the preacher. He
dislikes another part of the arrangement: "I would like to
spend more time with my grandchildren."

Vacations are scarce. He and Mrs. Parker try to get away
for a day or two once or twice a year. Jonah nourishes a
dream, however: "Most everyone looks forward to a week or
two off from work for vacations or time to just do nothing.
I'm saving up my time off. When the Lord calls me home, I'll
take it all at one time."

Jonah Parker offers this advice to anyone going into any
form of gospel ministry: "Get all the education and training
possible. Many of us did not have this opportunity."

Larry Salmons: Computer Programming
Manager and Pastor

Larry Salmons serves as pastor of the Bethel Baptist
Church near Cosby, Missouri, and is employed as a computer programming manager with the Heartland Health Sys-
tems. Bethel Church is a rural church with a resident
membership of 112 members. Pastor Salmons reports, "Bethel Church is growing spiritually as well as in number."

Larry gives this definition of a bivocational pastor: "A
man, called by God, who earns a living in a secular job as
he pastors a church, preaches at all opportunities, and ministers in the name of Jesus Christ." He sees unity in his life
though he has many responsibilities. He says, "For 168 hours
every week I am a Christian. Within this time frame I am a
husband, father, grandfather, father-in-law, shepherd,

preacher, counselor, advisor, and approximately forty hours a week I am a computer programming manager."

How does Larry's week go? Though it varies, an average week is something like this:

40 hours: job
20 hours: church and visitation
10 hours: sermon preparation
10 hours: other reading and studying
14 hours: family
 2 hours: recreation
 5 hours: ministering and counseling
10 hours: Bible study
uncounted hours for prayer

Pastor Salmons has discovered some advantages of being a bivocational pastor. One advantage is the opportunity of working with people in two settings: theological and work-a-day world. He says, "I get to share their joy from both, their despair from both, and their expectations for both."

He believes the church also benefits from the bivocational relationship. The people get involved in the ministry of the church because the pastor has limited time for the church. Larry also sees that his salary helps the financial responsibilities of the church. He sees his bivocationalism as a help instead of a burden to the church.

When asked for the disadvantages of being bivocational, he replies, "The disadvantages are minor compared to the advantages." One disadvantage that he does mention is a shortage of time for visitation.

Another disadvantage he has found is in the opportunities he misses. For example, since most meetings of his fellow ministers occur during the day, he misses opportunities of fellowship with them. Also, daytime training events are also not possible for him.

Larry misses opportunities to participate in associational, state convention, and national Convention activities. One reason is the lack of time to attend these meetings. But another reason he feels is the lack of an opportunity to participate in these meetings when he does go. He reflects: "Bivos are now appearing in associational programs and offices; maybe someday they'll be allowed to share their ministries on state and national levels."

Is he frustrated at the disadvantages and the many responsibilities? He testifies, "Out of all these time problems, God brings an effective and vital ministry—something we may not even understand ourselves."

Larry Salmons shares some needs he feels he has as a bivocational. The first one is "prayers, always." He also lists additional training. He desires more fellowship on the state and national level. He feels a need to be encouraged and recognized more as a bivocational by state and national church leaders.

The Reverend Larry Salmons is committed to bivocationalism. He says, "This is a vital ministry we are called by God to perform." He looks forward to seeing bivocationalism given a more prominent place in the attention and emphasis of the church.

Wayne O. Burkes: State Senator and Pastor

Wayne Burkes has been pastor of the Bolton Baptist Church of Bolton, Mississippi, for nineteen years. He has been in the Mississippi legislature for nine years. Prior to his election to the legislature, he was on the faculty of Hinds Junior College at Raymond, Mississippi. Wayne's pastoral ministry has always been bivocational. The Bolton Church has a resident membership of 140; they average 85 to 100 in Sunday School each week.

Senator Burkes has a flexible schedule. During the ninety days in January through March each year when the legislature is in session, the days are quite demanding. He also is a pilot and the chief of staff in the Mississippi Air National Guard with a rank of brigadier general. This responsibility requires some flying once or twice a week. Yet, he says, "I find that my different activities are very suitable so far as time management is concerned." He lives about half way between his office and his church.

What is a typical week like for this pastor? He says:

A typical week in my life is that my activities start at about 5:30 each morning and end about 10:00 or 10:30 at night. My days are spent in church visitation and hospital visitation, some legislative work, and I usually fly about one or two times per week.

Evenings are given to sermon preparation and family activities. Wayne confesses that his family often receives too little of his time. He makes an effort to be active in the local association and the state convention. His schedule allows him to attend the weekly Baptist pastors' conference about twice a month.

Wayne Burkes is a college and seminary graduate with an advanced degree in the secular educational field. Since he has never served a full-time pastorate, he is reluctant to speak of any advantages and disadvantages of the bivocational pastorate. However, he speaks of one factor that has both an advantage and a disadvantage to it. He says:

Being a bivocational minister does give me entrees to additional segments of society that has both advantages and disadvantages. The disadvantage is that I end up being the pastor to a lot of people who are not affiliated with our church or community who come to me because they know me through other settings.

The Reverend Burkes offers one word of advice based on his observations and experiences: "I think that there is a valid need for properly trained bivocational pastors." He has tried to follow that suggestion himself.

L. Homer Rich: High School Science Teacher and Pastor

Homer Rich serves as pastor of the forty-six-member Black Oak Baptist Church near Fayetteville, Arkansas. He recently left an eleven-year bivocational pastorate that grew to the point of wanting a full-time pastor. Pastor Rich resigned and accepted the Black Oak Church.

The Reverend Rich has this philosophy about his calling as a bivocational pastor. He believes every community needs a New Testament church witness and every church needs pastoral leadership. Since many churches can't support a full-time pastor, he concludes, "I am willing to be the 'tentmaker' if necessary."

When asked about the advantages to bivocationalism, Homer mentions the financial freedom of not having to depend upon the finances from the church for the needs of his family. A small church budget does not provide enough for adequate pastoral support. Homer also enjoys the relationship with his people in his pastorate, for "we see each other as co-laborers rather than the minister as a hired servant to do the people's ministry."

Management of time is a constant source of concern as Homer tries to work a schedule that must include the church, the home, and the high school classroom. He regrets being unable to attend associational and state church meetings, conferences, and training opportunities.

Homer Rich's weekly schedule during the school months follows a usual pattern. He drives twenty-three miles to school where he teaches six sections of chemistry, biology, and physics to about 125 students from about 8:00 AM to 4:00 PM. After 4:00 PM, Homer attends school committee meetings if necessary or visits in the hospital or homes. Each Wednesday he drives the twenty-seven miles from his home to the church for activities.

Thursday and Friday nights are often spent in school functions and responsibilities. He teaches in an adult GED program on Thursday nights and often has high school responsibilities at sporting events on Friday nights. Saturdays are given to doing needy home chores, and Sundays are spent at the church. He says, "The hospital visitation, other kinds of visitation, ministries in various homes, study time, and so forth are sandwiched wherever possible."

Pastor Rich plans time with his family. When his son plays football or basketball games at school, Homer attends. Concerning his family and church he says, "Serving the churches as pastor has been a family affair as our children have grown. Our family life is centered around the church, school, and family activities, such as travel and camping."

The Reverend Rich has been able to minister outside of his own church. He is active in the local Baptist association, having served on most of its committees from time to time. During school breaks and summers, he devotes a larger portion of his time to his church. He often finds time for some mission work, a revival meeting, or a religious conference somewhere.

What help does Pastor Rich feel the bivocational pastor needs? He says:

> Our Convention and agencies need to continue in the direction they are moving—recognizing the need for bivocational ministries, encouraging the work, and planning worthwhile fellowship and training experiences at times that are available to us.

Granville H. Watson, Jr.: Businessman and Minister

The Reverend Granville Watson, owner and president of Water Quality Science, Inc., of Moorehead, Mississippi, has had a varied ministry in bivocationalism. While an engineering student at Mississippi State University, Starkesville, Mississippi, he surrendered to God's call to the gospel ministry. He continued his studies at MSU, worked as a draftsman for Mitchell Engineering Company of Columbus, Mississippi, and served three small, rural halftime churches. He reflects, "It was here that I first saw the value of being bivocational."

Another bivocational pastorate was from 1964 to 1978 at the Moorehead Baptist Church of Moorhead, Mississippi, a church with about one hundred in attendance in Sunday School each Sunday. During this pastorate, Watson purchased eighty acres of land near Moorehead and began the Watson Catfish Farms, Inc.

Granville Watson has had two other types of bivocational experiences. He served the Sunflower County Baptist Association as bivocational director of missions from 1978 through 1984. In 1981 he established Water Quality Science, Inc. He says, "Because our product, AQUE-BACTA-AID, is being marketed worldwide, my ministry has expanded to sharing Christ with aquaculturists in all walks of life."

The Reverend Watson's present church work is yet another type of bivocational experience. He serves as a bivocational interim pastor of the Second Baptist Church in Greenville, Mississippi.

Granville sees a tremendous opportunity for bivocationals. He says:

> The great advantage to being bivocational is the exposure that I have to people in the marketplace of life. The work ethic of the Christian faith allows me to blend life-style evangelism and ministry into every minute of every day, in the office or at the church.

This opportunity for life-style evangelism is also the focal point for a disadvantage he sees. Watson says, "The biggest disadvantage is that people in our churches and 'full-time' pastors don't understand your great opportunity and the advantages of being bivocational."

A week in Watson's life includes time for each of his responsibilities. He is in his business office from 8:00 AM to 5:00 PM Monday through Friday of each week. Wednesday evenings and Sundays are given to church activities, visitation, and conferences. He prepares his sermons in the early mornings or the evenings. His wife works with him in the office in his business. They also plan quality time together as a family.

What needs does he have as a bivocational? He mentions acceptance first: acceptance and understanding by church people and fellow ministers. He also mentions "philosophy of ministry" as an area of interest and desire for greater understanding.

Granville Watson's bivocational pilgrimage has not been an easy one. When his first wife died, he had two little girls to care for. He then married his present wife, Becky, who had two sons. He and Becky have one child of their own. Together, they have worked out a fulfilling life. He says, "Our struggle to build a new life, deciding to be ourselves, and taking advantage of life's opportunities have all been a part in a fulfilling bivocational ministry and life."

Bivocationalism fits Granville and Becky Watson. This is how he feels about his dual roles as businessman and minister: "My ministry and my business are so natural to me that they made a wholeness or completeness to my life. I feel no conflict between serving God and making a living."

In conclusion, these men represent many other ministers who serve bivocationally today. They struggle with similar problems. They enjoy similar blessings. Many are happy and are finding fulfillment in both of their professions. God is blessing their ministries. They would not trade places with anyone. Bivocationalism is working in many communities in our time.

Note

1. This material comes from personal correspondence with these men and is used with their permission.

5

Understanding
the Philosophy

Is bivocationalism right or wrong? Is it a good way or a bad way to do ministry? These questions force us to search the Scripture for some answers.

We have already discovered a biblical basis for bivocational ministry in both the Old Testament and the New Testament. For example, Amos was a farmer/prophet and Paul was a tentmaker/preacher. No reference can be found in the Bible to disapprove or to criticize these two men for having secular jobs along with their call to ministry.

Paul experienced some criticism for making tents and refusing to accept money from the Corinthians (9:3 ff.). We do not know what was really behind this criticism. Paul defended not accepting money from the church as something he did so as not to hinder the gospel (9:12). Bivocationalism is not found to be wrong; rather, it is found as a way to be helpful in presenting the gospel to as many people as possible.

Fallacies Concerning Bivocationalism

Some people have objected to bivocationalism, saying that preachers should not serve the Lord and work at a secular job. Scripture has often been quoted to support this objection. One such verse is Matthew 6:24, where Jesus said, "Ye cannot serve God and mammon." The reasoning follows that a "full-time minister of God" can't serve a church and work for money at a secular job. Several fallacies can be found in this reasoning.

First, we should not equate serving God with serving a church only. We can serve God by serving faithfully in a secular job. Many laymen and laywomen do it every day. Second, we must not assume that a bivocational serves mammon any more than we assume that a church-supported pastor doesn't serve mammon. Ministers might be serving mammon, or they might not be serving mammon. Bivocationalism doesn't automatically mean that the preacher loves money. Maybe he loves bread on the table for his family. Maybe he loves to serve churches where church support is unavailable or inadequate. Matthew 6:24 can't be used to reject bivocationalism categorically.

Another objection to bivocationalism could be made from 1 Corinthians 9:14, "They which preach the gospel should live of the gospel." People who object to bivocationalism interpret this verse to say that the Lord or the church owes every preacher financial support that is adequate for full-time service. If you are truly called to preach, the Lord will supply your needs financially through a church or some religious organization.

One of the strongest cases put forth for church support of ministers is found in 1 Corinthians 9 where Paul defended his practice of self-support. Paul called the principle of church support a legitimate principle. Such illustrations as the soldier receiving necessary supplies, the vineyard owner living off the fruit of the vineyard, and the owners of flocks being fed by their animals' milk are given as reasons for church support (1 Cor. 9:7). Two Scripture passages about the ox not being muzzled while working and the farmers plowing and threshing in hope of a crop are added to Paul's argument of the principle of church support (1 Cor. 9:9-10). He further added that church support of the minister is reasonable and expected (1 Cor. 9:11). He even used the practice of the Temple priest eating the sacrifices brought by the people as a supporting reason for church support.

But then Paul said, "Nevertheless we have not used this power" (1 Cor. 9:12). Although church support of ministers is legitimate and biblical, church support might not be possible or available under certain circumstances. The right of church support might be rejected or refused by some ministers in order to fulfill a calling or meeting a need where church support isn't available. Church support is a right, but it is not automatic for every minister in every place of ministry.

Robert Lamb gave seven false assumptions often held by people who do not know much about bivocationalism.[1] These assumptions are as follows:

1. If a man will make a complete response to the call to preach, he is almost guaranteed a living from his church.
2. Inflation has brought on this recent idea of bivocationalism.
3. One only serves a bivocational pastorate as a step to something better and larger.
4. One only finds bivocational pastors in small country churches. These men are usually undereducated and marginally employed.
5. A bivocational pastor does not have enough time to be an effective leader.
6. The full-time pastor has more freedom to do great prophetic preaching than a bivocational.
7. One should not think of a bivocational as full-time.

Such fallacies should be cleared up in order to be able to see some theological aspects of bivocationalism.

Theological Aspects of Bivocationalism

Bivocationalism is being advocated by many church groups today. Can it stand the scrutiny of theology? Bivocationalism is a fact of life now, and it will probably be a fact of life in the future. How does it measure up to some theological beliefs?

No doubt the current wave of interest in bivocationalism has made church leaders study the concept. A. Donald Davies of the Episcopal Church explained this modern revival of the old tentmaker concept as follows: "Our Lord has launched again in our time a most exciting and renewing venture for ministry."[2] He concluded that bivocationalism "is a fully recognized, approved, and supported ministry equal with any other."[3]

Is it, however, theologically sound? Several theological considerations have a direct bearing upon bivocationalism. These considerations overlap to a great extent, but I want to present them separately.

Bivocationalism makes us look once again at the biblical teaching on the doctrine of the church. What is the church? Basically, a local congregation is a body of believers who has been saved and led together by the Holy Spirit to be the visible expression of the body of Christ in their area. Some have identified the congregation's purpose as worship, proclamation, education, and ministry. Christ is her Lord, and the Holy Spirit indwells her for leadership.

The church is fundamentally the people, not the preacher. The New Testament speaks of saints at Corinth, Ephesus, and Philippi. Vocational pastors came on the scene shortly after, but not simultaneously with, the birth of local congregations. Thus, the church functioned effectively without a highly organized and structured clergy for a number of years. Each Christian was gifted by the Holy Spirit for ministry, and these gifts were exercised under the Spirit's leadership.

Vocationally called clergymen were in the mind and plan of God for each congregation. God gave these leaders to the church in due time. But the church existed and functioned effectively before they arrived on the scene.

Therefore, it seems clear to me that we can have "church" without a resident, full-time, church-supported pastor living next door in the church's home. Baptists and Methodists have a heritage that includes the circuit rider who was the pastor of four or more smaller churches. He served them all through planned visits. Between visits the churches functioned under lay leaders.

Wayne Price told of his pastorates that were bivocational. He defined somewhat facetiously but realistically his responsibility: "A part-time pastor is a minister who is paid a part-time wage to produce a full church program with half the resources available to most other ministers."[4] All churches can have a full church program that is organized on the resources and opportunities of the congregation in light of God's purpose for a church. For some churches, a full-time resident pastor isn't one of its resources; a bivocational pastor is its only possibility.

A second theological consideration has to do with the biblical office called *pastor.* This office or calling does not appear in the New Testament fully developed. It took awhile for it to develop into the shape it has come to have in the Christian church. In the New Testament the names used for this office are often just adjectives describing activities performed by various church people.

The word *minister* means "to serve." The word *pastor* means "to shepherd." The word *priest* means "to offer sacrifices" and to serve in other religious capacities. The word *clergy* is a nonbiblical word that came on the scene later to designate official, vocational church leaders. The office of the minister developed over the years into what we have today.

Some of that development has been disproportionate. I refer to the fact that some believe that a minister should have one moral standard of life and that the laity can have another. Some church people believe that only the minister can pray for the sick, win the lost, adequately teach the Bible, and know the will of God for everybody. A church member often expresses it this way: "Pastor, we are here to help you do God's will." Where such ideas are held concerning the minister, the people feel that they cannot operate as a church without a full-time minister. The minister is needed to do the Lord's work while the people pay, pray, and praise him for his labors.

Bivocationalism wouldn't work under that kind of theology. Bivocationalism is best identified with the biblical teaching in Ephesians 4:11-12. In these verses the pastor is an equipper of the church people. He is "to prepare all God's people for the work of Christian service" (Eph. 4:12, GNB).

As an equipper the pastor works with and through his people. The work *of* the church goes on daily by the people. The work *on* the church goes on whenever the pastor can be with the people for service. If the pastor can be with the people full-time, good. If he can be with them only twenty-thirty hours per week, that is also good. The work of the church doesn't wait on the minister's physical presence but on his effective pastoral work of equipping. He does not have to live on the field or be church supported to perform this basic pastoral function. Though it might be ideal and even essential for a large church, it is not possible in every situation. The quantity of pastoral work might be limited in bivocationalism. But the quality and essence of pastoral work need not deminish one bit.

Many pastors and church leaders participate in what has been called a "shared ministry" concept of work. In this concept the pastor and the church leaders understand that they are to share responsibility for and work in the ministries of the church. The pastor isn't supposed to do it all. Neither are the church leaders and people supposed to do it all. Each one is to find his or her ministry according to personal gifts and the will of God. The pastor is to help each one find his or her place and work with each person in equipping and encouraging him or her in ministry. The goal is for the entire church to feel equal responsibility for God's will through that church. The pastor works with the people in sharing in the work of ministry through that particular body of Christ. This would be done whether bivocational or full-time.

Some churches object to bivocationalism on the grounds that a bivocational pastor does not have enough time to serve the church. Let's say that a full-time pastor has a church of six hundred members and the pastor works fifty hours per week as a pastor. That averages out to be five minutes per church member per week. A bivocational pastor, with a church membership of two hundred who works thirty hours per week as pastor, will average working nine minutes per church member per week. Theoretically, the bivocational pastor has almost twice as much time to spend per church member. If his primary work with each church member is equipping, the bivocational pastor in most churches might have more time available each week to spend with each church member than a full-time pastor would have with his larger church.

A third theological consideration is the matter of the stewardship of time and talents. Bivocational people are often multitalented. Dale Holloway observed that a bivocational pastor must be a smart man to be able to juggle the schedules of a church, a secular job, a family, his own personal plans, and keep everyone reasonably happy. John Elliott suggested, "The Dual Role Pastor generally fits the biblical pattern of the ten-talented person."[5]

If the average congregation on the North American continent has fewer than forty people at worship on a typical Sunday, what about the stewardship of time and talents of the pastor?[6] If he were full-time and worked a fifty-hour week as pastor, could he be challenged and find fulfillment during each of those fifty hours each week with a congregation of forty people?

This is not to suggest that small churches are unimportant. This is not to suggest that small numbers of people do not deserve the very best pastor in the world. Precisely because they do deserve the very best pastor bivocationalism is attractive to them. If a pastor serves full-time and has ten-talent abilities and isn't committed to bivocationalism, he will usually rise in the ranks to larger and larger churches. However, if he feels a call and challenge to two vocations (secular and church), he can serve a church that otherwise would never reasonably expect to be able to have him. He can give the church effective quality and experienced leadership and at the same time serve in a secular setting which also calls for his God-given abilities.

How much time is needed to do the essential tasks of an average church of forty worshipers? John Elliott spoke from the frustrations of his own experience the probing statement: "Pastors can correctly ask if mimeographing, shoveling snow, watching the furnace, or preparing a public supper manifests a faithful stewardship of abilities and gifts."[7] Bivocationals tend to do essential tasks because they are not available for the other many tasks that could be done.

Many dual-role ministers find that the secular job opens a challenging area of service to them. Counseling, teaching, serving as a lawyer, and many other vocations just might open more doors of ministry than a full-time pastor would normally have in a small church field. The bivocational can do his essential pastoral functions and also do his other secular functions which will call on all of his abilities and talents. Those nonessential pastoral duties can be done by others as expressions of their gifts, commitment, and time. Through bivocationalism God can place in the secular world a ten-talented dedicated person for service and witness. He can also place in a small church this same ten-talented person for ministry and leadership. Both areas benefit from the arrangement. In this way, the stewardship of time and talents is taken seriously and is practiced realistically.

Various writers and speakers have raised different theological considerations concerning bivocationalism. John Elliott, in his chapter "The Theological Bases of Dual Role," raised three basic considerations.[8]

First, Elliott asked if ordination to gospel ministry implied the exclusion of work in secular occupations or did it basically qualify one for work in religious matters along with other endeavors. Elliott's second consideration was whether full-time pastors of small churches exercise the best stewardship of their own talents and potential. The third consideration was a suggestion that bivocationalism fits well the New Testament doctrine of the priesthood of believers and the role of the laity.

Elliott's conclusions were that bivocationalism does not

violate ordination vows. He also suggested that many ministers have gifts and time available to be employed beyond the
pastorate. He contended that bivocationalism fits well the
doctrine of the priesthood of the believers and the biblical
expectations of the laity.

The CODE Project also studies this matter of the biblical
and theological bases for bivocationalism.[9] Their basic question was, "Does proper fulfillment of ministry in the name of
Jesus Christ require the commitment of total work time for
churchly duties by an ordained clergyperson?"[10] Their
findings led them to the conclusion that, whereas full-time
church duties are the normal practice, the teachings of the
New Testament and the practice of the early church do not
require full-time pastorates. Rather, Paul's example and the
examples throughout history indicate that bivocationalism
is a viable ministry. Need and opportunity have always been
factors in determining the style of ministry. No where is full
church financial support a prerequisite.

The theology of bivocationalism is very important and
needs further study. Financial need alone should not be the
decisive factor in whether a preacher or a church should be
bivocational. A sound, basic theology should undergrid the
practice. I suggest that the New Testament provides this
kind of theology.

Notes

1. Robert Lamb, "Bivocational Pastors Upset Treasured Assumptions," *The Tentmaker's Journal* (March-April 1980):5.

2. James L. Lowery, Jr., ed., *Case Histories of Tentmakers* (Wilton, Conn.: Morehouse-Barlow Co., 1976), p. iii.

3. Ibid., p. iv.

4. W. Wayne Price, "Redeeming the Time," *The Tentmaker's
Journal* (September-October 1980):7.

5. John Y. Elliott, *Our Pastor Has an Outside Job* (Valley Forge, Penn.: Judson Press, 1980), p. 24.

6. See Lyle E. Schaller, *The Small Church IS Different* (Nashville: Abingdon Press, 1982), p. 9.

7. Elliott, p. 24.

8. Ibid., pp. 21-22.

9. Clergy Occupational Development and Employment Project, *Dual-Role Pastorates* (Rochester: Clergy Occupational and Employment Project, 1978), pp. 1-4 and Appendix A-3.

10. Ibid., p. 1.

6

Counting the Pluses

Bivocationalism has a number of advantages in its unique approach to ministry. These advantages come to the bivocational minister, the minister's family, the local church he serves, his denomination, and his community.

Advantages to the Bivocational Minister

A bivocational minister wears several hats. Two of them relate to the minister's secular job and to his church work. He finds advantages to bivocationalism in each area.

SECULAR WORK

One plus in the area of the minister's secular job is the joy of having a fulfilling secular employment. Some ministers work in areas in which they have always had an interest. One pastor pursues his lifelong love affair with the newspaper business as he serves his bivocational church. Another man opens up a printing office of his own while he serves his church. Another man enjoys public school teaching along with his duties as pastor of his church.

Another plus is the satisfactory self-fulfillment of growing and succeeding in the secular job. Most secular positions are open for advancement. Competition is often keen. A bivocational minister can experience personal joy and fulfillment by successfully performing secular duties and advancing up the ladder of success.

Dr. Dale Holloway is a bivocational pastor. In the field of elementary education, he has advanced from a teacher to a state office position. He also has earned his Ed.D. in elementary education while serving in this secular position and also serving his bivocational church. A secular job doesn't have to be an uninteresting, boring job. It can be a source of pride and personal fulfillment like the work at the church.

A third plus is developing and enjoying friends and relationships outside the church. These friends often become some of the bivocational minister's closest friends throughout his life.

Some ministers find the secular training a definite plus to their work in their churches also. Seminars in selling, motivation, administration, and leadership provide insights for use in church work too. Many of these seminars are free of cost by virtue of his secular job. The full-time pastor would not normally have access to them.

CHURCH WORK

The bivocational minister knows the advantages of secular employment. He also is able to recognize several important pluses concerning his church work. Some of these are given here in summary form.

1. The bivocational minister is able to make an adequate living for his family. This is often impossible if the church is not financially strong.

2. He is available and able to serve a particular church by being willing to be bivocational. This same church might not otherwise be able to afford him financially.

3. He has a sense of independence and not a feeling of total dependence upon his church. If one vocation should fail, he has the other one for support.

4. He knows that he isn't putting a severe financial strain upon the church. They are not responsible for the total salary he must have to live on.

5. He often finds a welcomed diversion between his secular job and his church position. He leaves one area and moves to the other area, which is altogether different. This

allows him to keep a better perspective on both areas since he gets away from each one for a period of time each week.

6. Secular work often provides additional areas, situations, and opportunities for ministry and/or evangelism. He does not have to make himself leave his church office and enter the secular world to witness. He must do this five days every week. He finds many needs awaiting him that can be addressed each week.

7. Some bivocational ministers report that they gain a layman's perspective in doing secular work. Robert Dale testified, "I've discovered an important advantage in bi-vocational ministry. . . . When you preach and counsel and minister to laity, you know what it's like to walk in their shoes."[1]

8. The human distinction between the *secular* and the *religious* is often removed for the bivocational minister because of his two jobs. Dr. Wayne Oates said, "Being a bivocational minister has taught me that God's universe is a big place. It is not confined nor containable by any church walls, seminary walls, creeds, or kinship system."[2] Both jobs become avenues of Christian ministry.

9. A ten-talented bivocational person can avoid being underemployed by working two jobs. A small church often does not require a pastor's full week for ministry on the field. The secular job can provide another area for the expression of the minister's talents and abilities.

10. Many women are finding bivocationalism as the avenue for ministry as music directors, educational workers, youth directors, and other types of ministers. Often the door is not open to women for full-time positions. Many bivocational churches feel fortunate to have the services of a woman for staff positions.

These are some of the advantages being reported by many men as pluses to them in their church work and in their secular work. Bivocational pastor Maynard Head said, "Often a bivocational ministry has advantages, both to the pastor and to the church."[3] Let us look at some pluses to the family of a bivocational minister.

Advantages to the Bivocational Minister's Family

The bivocational minister's family can also find some advantages to being bivocational. These advantages help to offset the disadvantages that might be experienced.

For example, one solid advantage is financial. The family usually has greater financial security due to the two sources of income. The wife can often stay at home if she prefers and can be a homemaker. She might not need to work outside the home because of the two jobs of her husband. This is especially helpful when the family is young and small children are in the home. The father can be the sole breadwinner in the family.

In many cases the minister's mate will want to be employed outside the home. The family will have an even greater sense of financial security from their combined salaries.

A second advantage is the opportunity to own a home. A bivocational minister's tenure as pastor of the same church is usually longer than that of his full-time counterpart.[4] The children have the opportunity to stay in one community and grow up in the same house. This community becomes "home" to them. It also might be the place where the couple will retire. Owning their home usually makes the place feel more like home to the family.

A third advantage to a bivocational family is the security of an income coming in if either the secular job or the church position should fail. Secular jobs can fail and produce unemployment; also, church positions can fail. The Southern Baptist Convention reported that about twenty-five hundred Southern Baptist ministers are dismissed annually from their churches.[5] Two incomes can provide the family a security that one might not have with one job.

Some families find that not being on the pedestal or in the "goldfish bowl" of constant scrutiny a favorable fourth advantage. A community tends to treat the bivocational family a bit more like a regular community family. This is especially true when the family lives in a different community from the one where their church is located. The children escape that constant pressure of being under surveillance by some of the church members.

A fifth family advantage is one that has to do with teamwork. Some bivocational families treat their responsibilities at the church as a family effort. The wife serves as a team member. The entire family is often caught up in the opportunities of serving the church with their gifts and talents. The wife works closely with her husband, assuming some of the weekend responsibilities for him. The children get caught up in the weekend duties. This is true especially when the church is a mission church and much physical work needs to be done. Children can be responsible for helping with the chairs, hymnals, and other items involved in getting set up for Sunday services.

Each family must discover what fits it the best. Not all families would see such an opportunity for teamwork, but many families enjoy the work as a joint project. The children have meaningful experiences which will become good memories in years to come.

These advantages to the bivocational minister's family make this unique calling possible and meaningful to them.

Advantages to the Bivocational Church

A bivocational minister implies a bivocational church. There are several pluses to the church in this kind of relationship with its minister.

One advantage is found in the caliber of minister available to the church through bivocationalism. The church can have a trained minister because the minister will be able to provide some or most of his own salary himself. The church couldn't afford such a minister if it had to provide all of his support. The pastor can also live on the church field of his secular work is in the same area. Such a man can often improve the church's reputation as the community sees the church prosper under his trained leadership.

A second advantage has to do with the growth that often happens in the church. Because the pastor is not there all the time, the people must assume much of the work. The community begins to depend upon the church members for help and not upon the pastor alone. Such responsibility causes the people to grow faster in the Lord than they would if the pastor did all the ministry himself. A pastor who can organize his church for ministry and evangelism will see greater growth in the lives of the church members.

Another plus to a church is the identification the people often make with a "working pastor." People feel that he knows and understands them and their daily struggles. He is out there working with them. He works all week in the same world as they do. This causes them to feel that he knows more and understands their experiences better. Bivocationalism breaks down the barriers often experienced between the clergy and the laity. The pastor is seen as being more of a "real" person to them because of his secular job.

The church also receives a financial benefit. In a very small church, the minister will often give to his church more money in tithes and offerings than he will receive from them in salary. Some churches are able to pay a minister only from 10 percent to 50 percent of his total income. Thus, the pastor's offerings can prove to be life sustaining financially to a very small, struggling church.

Churches can give more money to ministry or missions by having a minister who is secularly employed also. Some of the money they would have had to pay a full-time minister can be redirected for ministry or missions. The church might not have the expense and upkeep of a pastor's home if the man already owns his home. Therefore, the budget isn't top-heavy with the pastoral salary allocation. The funds can be spread out to meet other needs in the church.

Churches are finding that by calling a bivocational pastor they can also call other bivocational staff members. Some churches have bivocational educational directors and music directors. Others have ministers to work in such areas as youth, senior citizens' work, Christian social ministries, and recreation. Sometimes the salary money required for one full-time minister can be used to call two or even three staff members who are all bivocational. The church benefits from having more trained leaders for the same amount of budget money.

Bivocationalism isn't for every church. Yet, for some it might be the best solution. Advantages like these help offset any disadvantages of not having a full-time minister on the field seven days a week.

Advantages to the Denomination

Are there any advantages to a denomination to have pastors serving in bivocational situations? Many denominations believe that there are pluses in this area.

The Southern Baptist Convention is emphasizing the beginning of new mission churches through bivocational church starters. These pastors go to an area where new churches are needed. They seek secular employment first. Then they begin to do survey work to find a core of people with whom to begin a new work. Many churches have been started through the labors of a man who was secularly employed also.

Denominations believe that bivocationalism might be the answer to strengthening weaker churches. Often the answer for such a church is trained, experienced pastoral leadership. Trained, inexperienced leadership might be inadequate for the needs of weaker churches. Bivocationalism permits a trained pastor to serve a small, financially weak church. He provides it with leadership necessary for growth.

Often a trained, committed bivocational pastor can give more quality leadership to a church than an untrained full-time person can give. The right kind of bivocational man might be the answer to helping these churches begin to grow. After a period of time both the pastor and the church can evaluate their ministry and decide whether to remain bivocational.

A third advantage to a denomination is in the area of denominational financial support. Bivocationalism can free money for use in denominational causes. A fair question to ask is, Does this church require several full-time staff members to accomplish its tasks? Or could some of them be bivocational? Money for personnel could then be directed into denominational needs.

I am not suggesting that full-time staff members are not important and essential to churches. A particular stage in a church's development might require full-time ministers. However, other churches function well with strong lay leaders who assume much of the work. The church employs bivocational leaders for counsel and direction. The effectiveness of the two kinds of church may be the same. The question of how many staff members a certain church needs is a legitimate and difficult question. Bivocationalism adds another dimension to finding the right answer for a particular church. By advocating bivocationalism, a denomination might strengthen its churches and free more money for other causes elsewhere.

Another advantage for a denomination to consider is found in the lay movement today. Many churches are seeing the emergence of the layperson to a place of more responsibility. Most denominations encourage this movement. Bivocationalism can be the arrangement whereby the limited availability of the bivocational pastor and the increasing availability of the layperson can complement each other in the church.

Advantages to the Community

The bivocational minister can be an asset to the community where he lives in several ways. The secular community gains a professional and a Christian in its work force. Secular employment sees people come and go. Some workers benefit a community. Some drain a community's resources, but most bivocational pastors should prove an asset to the work force in the community. They should be more stable. They care for the community, for its people, its problems, and its dreams and goals. Such workers improve the quality of the work force.

Another advantage to the secular community is the potential leadership skills available in the person of the bivocational. He is already the leader of a church. He might hold a secular position of management or leadership in his secular work, but he will also be potentially a leader in other worthy causes, drives, and projects.

A final advantage to a community lies in the area of small community dynamics. The smaller the community the more interrelated it is. Serving five days in the secular work force shows the minister the true conditions and the most pressing needs of the community. He is very interested in those things which affect his people. Helping meet community needs will mean helping meet his people's needs. Bivocationalism is an open door into vital community involvement. Communities need it and will find it a plus.

This chapter has been based on the premise that bivocationalism offers some advantages not found in a full-time ministry. No one is naive enough to suggest that there are no problems in this type of ministry. On the other hand, we must not automatically write it off as an unacceptable form of ministry either. Bivocationalism can well be the best answer for many ministers and churches today.

Notes

1. Robert D. Dale, "Hidden Advantages of Tentmakers," *The Tentmaker's Journal* (March-April, 1980):4.

2. Wayne Oates, "My Life and the Bi-Vocational Ministry," *The Tentmaker's Journal* (May-June 1980).

3. K. Maynard Head, "Linking Church and Pastor in a Rewarding Relationship," *Church Administration* (April 1981):44.

4. Gary Farley, "The Bivocational Minister," *Search* (Summer 1977):52.

5. Jim Lowry, "Dilemma Embarrasses SBC," *Facts & Trends* (February 1984):10.

7

Anticipating the Problems

Bivocationalism does have problems and limitations. All forms of ministry have their unique problems, and bivocationalism is no exception. These disadvantages are experienced by the bivocational minister himself, his family, his church, his denomination, and the community.

These problems are not mentioned to scare a person away from bivocationalism. Rather, they are honestly faced and discussed in an effort to forewarn a minister and to allow him to consider them realistically and prayerfully. Bivocationals everywhere are handling these problems successfully. A few no doubt succumb to them and leave the bivocational ministry.

Several surveys have been made among bivocationals, asking what they felt to be disadvantages in their calling. One group of about one hundred bivocational ministers in East Tennessee reported the following liabilities they had experienced: (1) discrimination by denominational leaders; (2) personal weaknesses seen by fellow workers in the secular job which hurt their testimony; (3) an independence which tempts them to run away and not deal with church problems; (4) falling into a rut in ways of doing things; (5) lack of time to serve the church as needed; (6) no time for fellowship with other ministers, and (7) shifting from the secular role to the church role.[1]

Doran McCarty of the Southern Baptist Convention, who follows closely the work of bivocationals, reported that several problems were regularly being voiced to him: (1) lack of time to be nothing more than a general practitioner instead of a specialist in counseling, administration, and the like: (2) identity problems since the bivocational isn't a full-time minister; (3) how to change churches when you can't change your residence; and (4) inability to take advantage of educational and training opportunities offered during secular work time.[2]

Perhaps it would be helpful to focus specifically on several areas where bivocationals seem to face problems. Not all men will experience all of the problems in every area. Yet, most of the problems continue to surface.

Disadvantages to the Minister Personally

One problem usually voiced is the problem of time. Bivocational pastors often find they do not have enough time for sermon preparation, church visitation, family responsibilities, and personal rest and recreation. Often the minister has his church, his secular job, and his family calling for time each day. Working out a daily schedule is frequently frustrating.

A second problem concerns the concept of role. Some bivocationals often wonder, Who am I? Am I a preacher, or am I a secular worker? Can I be a preacher if forty hours per week are spent at my secular job and only twenty to thirty hours are spent on church work? Wouldn't a real minister give all of his time to the Lord's work? Most denominational programming and emphasis for a minister is upon the full-time church and the full-time minister.

Another problem surfaces when the validity of bivocationalism come up for discussion. Is this a valid, legitimate ministry? If so, is it first class or at best second class? Single-vocational or full-time ministers might shun him, questioning his commitment to the church since he doesn't serve it all the time. Sometimes the full-time minister is jealous of the bivocational minister's financial possessions and his security.

Some bivocational ministers often wonder what they

could have accomplished if they had been full-time in a growing church. The drain on his energy from the forty-hour week at the secular job might leave little reserve for the church. At such times he is tempted to wish for just one vocation—the church—where all of his energies could be directed towards its welfare. A late call for pastoral help at night can't be compensated for the next morning by sleeping a little later.

Finally, the bivocational minister might not have a challenging secular job or an exciting church. If one or the other vocations is unrewarding, the man probably feels trapped. Surely, the question asked by most bivocationals from time to time is: "Is it worth it all?"

Disadvantages to His Family

The bivocational minister's family often faces problems also. They, too, suffer role identification. Are they a minister's family or a layperson's family? Sometimes they don't feel that they fit in either category.

The bivocational minister's wife misses many opportunities for fellowship with other ministers' wives because the bivocational isn't available for many meetings. Since he works at the secular job each day, the wife might be reluctant to participate with wives of full-time ministers in area meetings. Especially is this true when these meetings involve both husband and wife.

Another's problem is the absence of the husband and father from the home due to two jobs. Unless the husband and wife follow strict guidelines acceptable to both, the husband can be out of the home most of the time. An absentee father is an absentee father, regardless of the reason.

One other area of difficulty is the coordination of the calendar with two or three jobs to consider. When will the family take a vacation? If the mother also works outside of the home, how can father and mother be off at the same time? As children get older with their own schedules of events, the problem can get very sticky, to say the least. Yet, hundreds of bivocationals face these matters and work out acceptable solutions each week.

Disadvantages to the Church

Some churches have reported problems in being a bivocational church. These problems are not necessarily insurmountable, but they are nonetheless real to many congregations.

Often the minister is unavailable to minister to a person or family immediately when the minister's presence might be expected. The minister might be working at his secular job miles away from the church field. Therefore, he probably can't visit the person or family until he gets off from work or even until he returns to the church community on the weekend. Other church leaders can step in and minister, but many families want the pastor there when they need him.

A second problem unfortunately is real to some churches who have bivocational pastors. He is a preacher only and not a shepherd/leader of the flock. He comes to the church, preaches at the stated times, and does very little pastoral visitation, counseling, or administration. The people long for a shepherd to minister to them.

This problem isn't limited to bivocationalism by any means. The full-time congregation might have the same situation with a particular minister who is "incomprehensible on Sunday and invisible during the week." The problem is with the minister, not a type of ministry. A bivocational has to give extra attention to utilizing what time he is on the church field to minister to his people. Counseling and administration go along with preaching.

A third problem lies in the area of status. Churches, like preachers, generally want to be full-time churches. Older churches remember the days when they shared a preacher with one, two, or even three other churches. Southern Baptists had what they called quarter-time churches. One minister served four churches. Each church had preaching once a month. Today, the ideal for many is a man full-time, living on the church field. If for some reason the church can't have this, it might feel second class, or less than ideal.

Tenure of the pastor is another potential problem area for a church. Short pastorates plague some churches. Pastorates that last past enthusiasm and commitment on the part of the people and the pastor often get into trouble. "Where there is no vision, the people perish" is true for both churches and preachers. This problem is a pastor problem or a church problem, not one unique to either bivocational or full-time pastorates. A bivocational pastor must guard against becoming complacent or preoccupied with his secular work and failing to give positive leadership to his church. He must not let his church be anything but full-time in his commitment and implementation of the will of God through him among the people.

Disadvantages to the Denomination

Most denominations are earnestly committed to all of their pastors and churches, regardless of size, strength, or location. However, working effectively with bivocational pastors has some disadvantages.

Bivocational ministers aren't available for day meetings during the week. They have to be on their secular jobs. They can't attend the Monday morning pastors' conference or daytime regional or state meetings. In order of priority, a denominational meeting would come fourth on the list behind the home, the church, and the secular job for most bivocationals. Therefore, bivocational pastors are not as involved in denominational affairs as their full-time counterparts.

Denominational programs are not important to some bivocationals. They figure they can't participate in these programs because they don't have time or won't be available. Bivocationals try to lead their churches in basic ministries. But extra programs or projects might be omitted or ignored due to the bivocational ministers' schedules. Thus, cooperative efforts among churches often do not involve bivocational churches. The denomination isn't able to have the participation and resources from these churches that is desirable.

Denominations often do not get as much financial support for denominational causes from bivocational churches as they do from a full-time church of the same size. A study made by the Southern Baptist Convention revealed that, in matters of finances, the per capita giving by bivocational churches was lower than in full-time churches of the same size.[3] This included per capita receipts, per capita home mission gifts, and per capita total mission gifts. The report observed:

> This is not surprising since the churches with bi-vocational pastors are smaller in size. This does tell us something about the financial situation of the churches that use bi-vocational pastors and should certainly be taken into consideration when doing planning and programming for these churches.[4]

In other areas of the study, the bivocational church often did better than its full-time counterpart. Bivocational churches led in the rate of baptisms, rate of total additions, and the rate of average Sunday School weekly attendance. Rates or percentages are often higher in the smaller church.

Disadvantages to the Community

A few complaints are voiced by the people in the community concerning the bivocational minister. Some people sincerely believe that a God-called preacher shouldn't work outside the church. When one does, he is often under suspicion at first and might be resented. Some people feel preachers should "stay in their place." A few would feel threatened having to work beside a preacher every day. Others might feel threatened by the minister's training and skills. Many times this resistance can be overcome through patience and thoughtful conduct by the minister.

Some businessmen and company officials have disapproved of bivocationals in the secular work force when the ministers abused their secular jobs by "preaching" all the time to the other workers rather than working at the job. Whereas a Christian is always to be a witness for Christ, one must learn appropriate times and ways to practice aggressive, verbal witnessing. The secular job deserves 100 percent commitment and the highest quality of work possible. Most bivocationals quickly learn what should and shouldn't be done on the job. A few have not been able to fit in and have had to leave secular jobs.

Another disadvantage that is expressed sometimes by the community is the hurt, disappointment, and even disillusionment felt when a minister doesn't live up to the expected moral standards of the ministry. Community people may not always listen to preachers, but they usually expect them to live and act like preachers should. When a minister doesn't "practice what he preaches," the devout are hurt and offended and the skeptics have a field day. The opposite is also true when the minister lives like the salt and light of God's kingdom. He is a blessing to any community.

A last disadvantage in many communities has to do with the problem of time and availability. The bivocational minister might not live in the community. Even when he does, he has limited time for community activities due to his church and secular responsibilities. Therefore, he is oftentimes unable to be as active as he might otherwise be in the life of the community where the church is located. The community misses the contribution that he could make, and the minister misses the contribution that a community can make in his ministry. This disadvantage presents a challenge to the bivocational minister to find some ways to be involved in the community as much as his time and talents allow.

This has been a rather forthright discussion of the problems voiced concerning bivocationalism. By no means does this imply that all bivocationals experience all of these problems all of the time. This discussion does imply, however, that this calling is not an easy one. Many, however, confess that bivocationalism requires a ten-talented man. Probably not all preachers are talented or gifted by temperament

8

Handling the Problems

Bivocational pastors have the same general responsibilities in their pastorates as all other pastors. However, the bivocational minister probably focuses specifically on several of these responsibilities and gives priorty to them.

What are some of these responsibilities? Two studies have been done with two groups of bivocational pastors on how they use their time in a normal week. One study was done with ninety-five Alabama bivocational pastors. This study revealed the following division of time:[1]

Secular Work	37.07 hours per week
Personal/family time	10.91 hours per week
Sermon preparation	6.96 hours per week
Bible study, prayer	6.80 hours per week
Leading church services	5.23 hours per week
Soul-winning visits	3.55 hours per week
Visiting the sick	3.11 hours per week
Visiting prospects	2.32 hours per week
Other church activities	2.07 hours per week
Counseling	1.97 hours per week
Church administration	1.45 hours per week
Denominational activities	0.95 hours per.week

A second study was done with one hundred Tennessee bivocationals. These ministers spent their week in church activities as follows:[2]

Studying the Bible, prayer	8.1 hours per week
Preparing sermons	5.8 hours per week
Witnessing	5.7 hours per week

Visiting the sick	4.0 hours per week
Leading in worship	3.6 hours per week
Counseling	2.1 hours per week
Committee meetings	1.5 hours per week

In the Alabama group, the pastors averaged 37.07 hours per week in their secular work. If we subtract personal/family time and Bible study/prayer time, they spent about 27 hours per week in their church duties. The Tennessee group averaged about 22 hours per week if we delete studying the Bible/prayer time. If this Bible study were related to preaching, both groups spent more hours on church duties in an average per week.

What responsibilities must a bivocational pastor fulfill each week in his church? These studies indicate that he must study, prepare sermons, visit, witness, lead in worship, counsel, and attend meetings. How does he manage it all? What suggestions might be helpful concerning these activities?

Suggestions Concerning Weekly Ministries

STUDY AND SERMON PREPARATION

A pastor who serves only a church and has no secular work might give each morning of the week for study and sermon preparation. He might study Monday through Wednesday and then zero in on sermon preparation from the middle of the week until Sunday. A bivocational pastor must utilize short periods of time throughout the week for study and sermon preparation. Some get up earlier in the mornings for study. A few can study some during the lunch break. Others might study late at night after the children go to bed. Time can be found on Saturdays and early Sunday mornings or Sunday afternoons. Some can study during the Sunday School hour before morning worship and the hour prior to the evening worship service. If the pastor must spend time each day driving to and from work, he might listen to study tapes in his car.

Ideally, studying the Bible and other subjects for personal growth and studying for sermon preparation should be separated. Often studying in one area will lead to study in the other.

How do you find the time for study and sermon preparation? Robert Lamb shared some suggestions.[3] He served as a college professor and also served a church as pastor. Lamb's first suggestion was to work with your body's rhythms. When are you the most alert and productive? Some are more alert in the morning; some, at night. Find your best time and schedule your most difficult and important study tasks at that time if at all possible.

Lamb also suggested that pastors secure good resources. Pastors need to secure books that provide the most help. An expository preacher would have a different library from one who does topical preaching predominantly. You might find a church nearby that has a good library. In it will probably be several sets of commentaries and other books. You could check these out to see if they are profitable to you. Then you could purchase the ones that give you the most help.

Lamb also urged that pastors set realistic study goals. Most pastors know of areas in their ministry where additional study needs to be done. Maybe it is in counseling or church administration or theology. Whatever the area of need, pastors can set some kind of reading schedule for the year. They can be on the lookout for seminars on these subjects that will be offered nearby. They also can find helpful correspondence courses. Lamb lamented that a busy work-and-church schedule keeps many bivocationals from being able to attend the training events. He concluded that in the area of study and training, "We've got to do a lot of it alone. It is almost impossible for classes and training events to be placed at times when all can attend." The advantage to securing study and training alone is the flexibility to tailor the study programs to fit individual needs.

VISITATION AND EVANGELISM

A second major area of church responsibilities is visitation. Every pastor must visit the sick, the lost, and the regular church people. The Alabama bivocational pastors mentioned earlier in this chapter spent an average of 8.98 hours per week in various kinds of visitation. The combined total among the Tennessee pastors, also mentioned earlier, was 9.7 hours per week spent in witnessing and visiting the sick. These totals might seem high unless they include time spent witnessing on the secular job and that which was done among the lost on the church field.

Maynard Head, a bivocational pastor in Kentucky who also serves as vice-president of a college, has written of his frustrations and efforts to find time to visit the people whom he should visit. He offered two suggestions on how to minister to the flock. He urged first that the congregation and church leaders be educated in ministry and trained to care for each other. Then he shared his own personal visitation program.[4]

Church members need to be informed of their responsibility to care for one another. Sermons can be preached on this theme. Training sessions can be conducted at the church to prepare and assure Christians that they can minister to each other effectively. Hospitals will often have a leaflet on how to visit hospital patients. These leaflets can be secured, read, and then discussed in a training session.

Maynard Head also encouraged the use of deacons in the pastoral ministries role. Many denominations have training courses for deacons on visitation and other forms of ministry. Several hour-long sessions over a period of a few weeks will offer valuable training for deacons. Some of them will pick up on it eagerly and become skilled at making helpful visits.

Whom should the pastor visit? Head suggested that the pastor make selected visits and assign the less serious visits to others. The pastor needs to visit those who are seriously ill or those who are having surgery. Some hospital patients can be seen early in the morning before the pastor goes to the secular job. In some areas, a short visit can be made during the lunch hour or on the way home from work.

Head made soul-winning visits with a layman on Saturdays. This adds strength to the visit and offers a training opportunity with the layperson. Some visits, however, must be made alone. Another person would hinder the process. At times Head planned an evening for visitation.

The bivocational whose secular job takes up eight hours a day has only the nights and the weekends for visitation unless he can get off from work for emergency visits. Therefore, visitation must be planned during the available time. Emergency situations cannot be programmed. Pastors have to go when they arise. But other kinds of visitation can be planned. Many pastors keep a list of their church members and note on this list when the visits are made. Prospects and lost people can also be kept on a list, and the visits made with them noted and filed. Through a planned approach, more people can be visited and all people who need to be seen will be contacted.

Many visits must be made in person. But for some a phone call or a note is also very effective. Some follow-up visits can be made over the phone. A call or a note of encouragement is often as effective as a personal visit. The bivocational will not have time to do everything in the area of visitation. He will have to mobilize others and plan his own program of visitation.

COUNSELING

Another area of responsibility as a bivocational pastor is that of counseling. People need to talk to the minister. A bivocational pastor isn't able to announce a daily schedule when he will be in his study and available for formal counseling sessions. His time probably won't allow that. He will have to schedule counseling sessions as he is available.

Many times counseling sessions can be planned around

the worship services at the church. The person might come thirty minutes or an hour early to talk to the minister. Or the person might remain for a period of time following a service. Sometimes a counseling session can be conducted during the Sunday School hour or during the time some organization is meeting. Sunday afternoon is also a possibility for a counseling session at the church or in the person's home.

Most pastors aren't equipped to do long-term counseling with their members. Such counseling requires specialized training. But all pastors must and can do effective short-term work. They need to counsel with youth, with young couples, with individuals who experience tragedy in their lives, and with couples who plan to be married or who are considering divorce. Every church needs to be able to have its pastor available sometimes for conferences.

The bivocational pastor can plan his schedule when he will be available at certain times to talk with people. He can announce it or put it in the bulletin. The pastor's wife can also be alert to opportunities for unscheduled counseling situations. The pastor can also encourage laypersons in the church who have counseling skills to be available to help others. Many people just need someone to listen and understand. Others need more professional help. The pastor will need to do counseling himself and also equip others to share in this ministry.

Sometimes a person or family can drive to the pastor's home if he lives within a reasonable distance. Some people like to keep counseling sessions secret from the community if possible. Being willing to take some cases in the home will make the pastor available to some people in their time of need.

The bivocational pastor can utilize community resources for counseling. Often a fellow pastor is skilled and might be available for a referral. Usually secular agencies and possibly religious agencies to which the pastor can refer his members are nearby. In this way he can help them get counseling without doing all of it himself.

ATTENDING MEETINGS

There are always meetings ministers should attend: church meetings, denominational meetings, and community meetings. No one is able to attend them all. Therefore, priority must be given to those meetings deemed mandatory, and those meetings must be attended. Sometimes, someone else can represent the pastor or the church at a meeting.

Many ministers try to schedule all church meetings on Wednesday and Sunday when many people are at church. Meetings are arranged to meet prior to a service or after a service. If the bivocational can be with the church only on Wednesday and Sunday, all meetings which require his presence must be on those two days. Through delegation and lay leadership, the pastor can organize his people so that the pastor won't need to attend every committee in the church that meets.

Suggestions for a Weekly Schedule

WORKING UP A SCHEDULE

Puting all of this together isn't easy. The schedule and demands will not be the same each day. Each bivocational minister's situation will probably differ from anyone else.

Paul M. Broyles served as bivocational pastor of the Pleasant Grove Baptist Church, Limestone, Tennessee. He reported that his daily schedule usually included two hours of Bible study and prayer from 5:00 AM to 7:00 AM, several evenings for prospect visitation, Sunday afternoons for church members and homebound person visitation, and Friday nights for his family.[5]

Richard Hill served in Montana in a bivocational pastorate before attending seminary. The Reverend Hill shared his daily schedule:

8:00 AM - 4:00 PM	Secular work
4:00 PM - 6:00 PM	Family time
6:30 PM - 9:30 PM	Church work, such as hospital

and home visitation
9:30 PM - 10:00 PM   Family and children
10:00 PM - Midnight   Sermon preparation

Deacons in the church were used for visitation when a visit by the pastor was not possible.[6]

In setting up a schedule a bivocational pastor could plan a calendar of activities for a week. He would need to consider such things as:

Secular work schedule
Family and personal schedules
Church responsibilities
Community responsibilities

He could begin by listing his secular work schedule on the days when he is employed in this work. It might be from 8:00 AM - 5:00 PM Monday through Friday of each week. Those hours would be inflexible. Church responsibilities which are also inflexible should be written in next. These would include definite responsibilities of the church, such as leading in worship and prayer meeting.

Next, the pastor could list the family, personal, and community responsibilities to which he is committed. Some of these activities might also be inflexible. When all of these are listed for each day on a weekly calendar, the pastor can then see what hours remain in which he has some freedom to schedule whatever he determines to be important.

For example, he might see that he has from 5:00 AM until 8:00 AM most mornings for activities if he so chooses. He also might have from 5:00 PM until bedtime available many nights for activities. Saturdays and Sunday afternoons might also be flexible. He would know that he has freedom to use these periods of time each day or each week as he sees fit. It would be these blocks of time into which he could schedule activities which are not already scheduled. Each week needs to be considered separately because schedules and demands will vary.

Here is how I tried to organize my week during a period when I served a church as pastor and also taught full-time at a seminary. My plan was unique to me, but the principles involved seem to be general ones that all bivocationals work with in some way.

I tried to give about twenty-eight hours per week to the church and the remaining hours to my other job and to myself and family. Here is how my schedule went.

1. On Tuesday, Wednesday, Thursday, and Friday I was responsible for work at the seminary, for time with my family, and for whatever personal time that was available. During these four days I sought to find as much time as possible for sermon preparation. Study time was found either early in the mornings or at night after work.

2. On Wednesdays I left around 4:00 PM to drive seventy-five miles to the church for Wednesday night activities. Church activities that involved me were from 7:00 - 8:00 PM. From 5:45 PM - 7:00 PM I could do any number of things. I could make a necessary hospital visit, have a counseling session at the church, visit a home, have a committee meeting before prayer meeting, do administrative things in the office, or study. After prayer meeting was over at 8:00 PM, I could have a committee meeting, a counseling session, or make a visit. Then I would drive home, getting there around 10:00 PM.

Because the bivocational must do things when he finds time available, this schedule for Wednesday nights allowed me to do what needed to be done on a particular week. If no emergency existed, such activities as making visits, being available for counseling sessions, having committee meetings, or short periods for study could be planned for Wednesday nights.

On Saturdays and Sundays I spent some time on the church field. I tried to put in a minimum of four and one-half hours of church work on Saturdays. That work was usually visitation, administration in preparation for Sunday, or sermon preparation. Since we had a place to spend Saturday night on the church field, usually several more hours were spent on Saturdays doing church-related things. However, several hours were also given to rest or family activities on that day.

4. On Sunday I tried to be available from 9:00 AM to 10:00 PM for church activities. By getting to the church office by 9:00 AM, I could spend forty-five minutes before Sunday School in more study for the sermon, in administration in the office, or in making a necessary short visit with someone in the local hospital. Some counseling sessions were also conducted at that time.

Sunday School and worship services were from 10:00 AM to 12:00 noon. I was free from 10:00 to 11:00 during Sunday School to do whatever was needed. Usually the times was spent in last-minute study on the sermon. Sometimes a counseling session was scheduled or a soul-winning session was planned with a Sunday School member who was already to accept Christ. Then at 11:00 AM we had our morning worship service.

Sunday afternoons from around 1:00 PM to 5:00 PM were given to some rest, visitation, study, committee meetings, or administration. The needs varied. But if nothing were pressing or scheduled, some visits could be made. Since we had a churchwide training program at 6:00 PM each Sunday night, we scheduled committee meetings prior to that hour. That is when we had our deacons' monthly meetings.

The 6:00 PM hour was like the Sunday School hour. I was usually free to do what was needed. I could get in forty-five minutes of study, counseling, or administration. From 7:00 to 8:00 PM we had our evening worship service.

From 8:00 to about 9:00 PM before I left the church field to return to my home, I had an hour for a visit or for a committee meeting if one were scheduled. I arrived home around 10:00 PM.

Generally the number of hours spent in church work each week was something like this:

1. Monday through Friday   5-8 hours
   (This was sermon preparation time.)
2. Wednesday   6 hours

(This included the trip to and from the church plus the time spent on the field.)

3. Saturday   4 1/2 hours
(This included the trip to the field and the hours actually worked.)

4. Sunday   13 hours
(This included the trip back home.)

If you are a bivocational pastor you know that nobody is able to have such a cut-and-dried schedule as I have given. Emergencies come up, and your best plans have to be put aside. Funerals and weddings usually require additional times. Associational meetings are extra if they are attended. But most of you have some general schedule that you try to keep. It takes constant attention to be able to give proper time to yourself, your secular job, your family, and your church. You have to use the available time as wisely as possible.

Any pastor must work out his priorities and then delegate some of the work in the church to others. What might be a bivocational pastor's priorities? Obviously this answer will vary from pastor to pastor. However, all pastors must preach, pastor the flock, be an administrator in church leadership, and counsel with the people as needs arise in their lives. Many pastors put these four items in the order mentioned. Others vary the positions according to their priorities in ministry.

As a bivocational pastor you have agreed to preach two or three sermons per week in the church. You have agreed to pastor the flock, visit the sick, visit the members, and seek to reach the prospects and the lost. You have also agreed to be an administrator in the leadership of the church by providing overall leadership to the church programs. You have also agreed to counsel and to see people as needs and opportunities arise. In addition to these matters, you have agreed to be available as much as possible for funerals, weddings, and other activities that are involved in serving a church.

Performing these functions requires the setting up of what

you consider to be priority functions for your ministry. Preaching is usually a priority function. Unless you share this responsibility in a multistaff relationship, you are the sole one responsible most of the time for three sermons each week. You usually can't delegate this function. Therefore, you make preaching a top priority.

Serving as a pastor to your flock is also an essential function. Others can serve the flock, but no one can take the place of the pastor. Most churches call you to preach and to pastor the flock. Therefore, you must work out some way to fulfill this activity as faithfully as possible.

Since the flock will need more ministry than even a full-time pastor can possibly give, the pastor can delegate some of this ministry to others. He can help his church become a caring people. He can urge and teach his classes and organizations to minister to their members. The deacons and other church leaders can also be trained to provide ministry to the church family. Part of the monthly meeting of the deacons can be spent sharing the needs of the church and community and what has or can be done to meet these needs.

Serving as the administrator in the overall leadership of the church can be done effectively through a monthly church council. This council is composed of all of the leaders of the church. The pastor serves as chairman. He calls the leadership together to plan and evaluate everything that is being done in the church. Most things being done in a church are being done by an organization, a committee, or a church leader. The pastor has the things that he does. Each organization, committee, or church leader has the things that he or she is to do. The church council coordinates all of these matters and enables everyone to work together to accomplish what the church believes God wants it to do.

The church council provides the pastor a handle by which to delegate church activities that he doesn't have time to do or maybe doesn't need to be doing. Through mutual planning and coordination, the council can see that each activity has someone or some organization responsible for it. The council recommends its plans and projects to the church for approval. Then, it represents the church when it meets for reports, further implementation, and evaluation.

Through the church council meetings, and the pastor can constantly remind the church leadership of his personal priorities. He can help them to see that he can only do certain activities in the twenty to thirty hours a week that he gives to the church. The council can find someone else to be responsible for the work or postpone it until someone can be found to assume it. God has many gifted and talented people in the church who need to be enlisted for service. In the bivocational pastorate, these people are needed more obviously than in any other place.

During a church council meeting, the pastor might lead the council to list all of the things it thinks ought to be done in and by the church. The pastor could list them on a chalkboard. The list should include such matters as cleaning the church, turning on and off the lights, printing the bulletin, ordering supplies, cutting the grass, and all of those matters that tend to be overlooked.

Then the pastor could lead the council to suggest what person, organization, or committee should be responsible for each of the things that it feels ought to be done. The council members would probably list the pastor as the one who should preach the sermons each week. The Sunday School director would surely be listed as the one to lead the Sunday School. Many of the items on the chalkboard will be obvious as to whom the responsibility should be given. However, many of the items might not have an obvious person or group to whom responsibility could be given. At this point the pastor doesn't want the council to give him these items as his responsibility. He must constantly remind them of the limited number of hours he has and of the priority activities he must do in those hours. Much misunderstanding and false expectations can be avoided from such an open discussion among the leaders of the church.

When the church council determines the activities and the

ones responsible for each activity, it should make a report to the church for approval and information. The church will know what the bivocational pastor will seek to do himself and what he will lead others to do.

Monthly meeting of the church council and business meeting become times when the leadership and the church are reminded of who is responsible for what. Everybody is on the team, but each one has his or her own assignments. This is one method by which a bivocational pastor can have his priority assignments and then delegate the other matters to the appropriate person or persons in the church.

A helpful tool for a church council and pastor to use in understanding and assuming responsibilities is a "Covenant for Ministry."[7] A copy of this covenant can be found in the Appendix. In this covenant, the pastor and the church members work out an agreement as to who will do what in the church. In twenty-three ministry areas, the pastor and people both make commitments of time and responsibility, according to an agreed schedule. Such a convenant should prevent false expectations of the pastor from the people. Also, working through this covenant will help the church leaders to be aware of the ministries for which they need to assume leadership and responsibility.

Problems can be recognized and handled. They can't be prevented unfortunately, but they can be dealt with realistically and honestly. Both pastor and people must work together and keep lines of communication and understanding open.

Notes

1. J. T. Burdine, Jr., "Alabama Bivocational Pastors Survey Summary," 1 October 1980. An unpublished report.
2. Gary Farley, "The Bivocational Minister," *Search* (Summer 1977): 54.

3. Robert Lamb, "Getting There on My Own," *The Baptist Program* (June-July 1982): 8.

4. K. Maynard Head, "Pastoral Visitation and the Bivocational Minister," *Church Administration* (March 1981): 43-44.

5. "Paul Broyles: Bi-vocational: A tale of two works," *The Maryland Baptist,* 4 November 1982, p. 3.

6. An interview with Richard Hill on the campus of New Orleans Baptist Theological Seminary.

7. See Appendix for copy of "Covenant for Ministry."

9

Training the Pastor

Most churches believe in a trained clergy. Some churches will not ordain a minister until he has completed his college and seminary education. Most congregations desire an educated minister as their pastor.

However, not all ministers have opportunity to prepare themselves as they would prefer. Some men are called to ministry early in life. They can go to college and seminary and then begin their service in a church. Others are saved and/or called to ministry later on in life. These ministers face a difficult situation as they look at four years of college and three years of seminary before they can work in their first church. Therefore, some of them do not go to college or seminary. They begin work with a church and educate themselves along the way through formal and informal methods.

In considering the training of a bivocational minister, we might consider three different groups of people who need to be trained. One group is composed of those who plan to be bivocational from the start and have time and opportunity to go to college and seminary. These ministers can prepare for the secular field in college and the church vocation in seminary. Another group is made up of men who are already trained in either the secular or the religious field when they feel called to bivocational ministry. These will need preparation in the field that is lacking. The last group is made up of those who for one reason or another have little formal education beyond high school and who have limited opportunity to obtain it. These people need help in finding educational training on both a formal and an informal basis.

Bivocational ministers need a particular kind of education. Many educational institutions and church leaders are moving in this direction to help students prepare specifically for bivocational ministries. Seminaries are responding more and more to this need.

The CODE Project, conducted in New York in 1975-1978, was an exploration of dual-role pastorates in four denominations of Western New York. That study included a survey of theological seminaries in the United States made by the Reverend Thomas Little as part of his Doctor of Ministry degree requirements at Colgate Rochester Divinity School. Little wanted to "ascertain their [the seminaries] interest in, and development of programs for Dual-Role ministries."[1]

Little found eight seminaries where students could do work on a career in a secular field while working on their theological education.[2] These dual-competency programs involved study at a nearby cooperating university where the student could obtain training in such fields such as law, social work, education, health, music, counseling, administration, library science, and communications. On the completion of study in these dual competency programs, a student had met the full academic requirements for two professions. For example, he might be at the same time qualified as a minister and an elementary school teacher.

Other seminaries are responding in different ways to the need for training the minister specifically with bivocationalism in mind. Special courses on the bivocational minister are offered from time to time. Some seminaries have bivocational courses as a regular part of the curriculum. The ministerial student is introduced to the bivocational ministry through lectures, testimonies by visiting bivocational ministers, reports by denominational workers who work in this field, and materials prepared by the denomination on opportunities and procedures for entering a bivocational ministry. Correspondence courses are also available to bivocational ministers who already serve on the field.

Bivocationalism seems to be a needed specialized form of ministry today and in the future. How could one prepare himself specifically with a bivocational ministry in mind?

Much of the student's planning would depend on when he decides to go the bivocational route. If he makes that decision early in college, then he can prepare for the secular vocation in college and the church vocation in seminary. For example, he could graduate from college qualified in education or some other secular field. Then he would attend seminary for preparation in church ministry.

If a student is in seminary when he begins to prepare for a bivocational ministry, he must work out a plan for preparing himself for two vocations. Several possibilities are available. Some seminary students have college training that will be valuable for a secular vocation. These students can upgrade or build on the college work with additional study. One seminary student found that he needed only a few additional college courses to qualify for certification in education. He took those courses at a nearby university at night while completing his seminary studies.

Some seminary students have skills they developed before entering the ministry which can be used for the secular vocation. These skills can be employed immediately upon graduation. Skills such as that of a carpenter, a mechanic, or some other kind of work provide many bivocationals with their secular vocation. These skills can be updated or advanced through further education in night classes, summer courses, or through an additional year of vocational training following seminary.

Some seminary graduates will return to the university to prepare for the secular vocation. One seminary graduate entered law school following seminary graduation in order to prepare himself for bivocational ministry as a lawyer and a pastor. Those three years invested in law school will pay off over the next twenty years of bivocational ministry. In many denominations, the student can be serving a nearby student pastorate while preparing himself educationally for bivocational ministry later.

The bivocational minister who is unable to attend college or seminary can pursue his educational training and ministry preparation in the ways that are open to him. Each person's situation will be different, but most will find such opportunities as:

1. College night or weekend classes,
2. Denominational seminars or various subjects relative to the local church and its work,
3. Correspondence courses from the denomination or from other religious institutions,
4. Tapes, books, videos, and other training materials,
5. Educational and religious television programming designed for the church and church leaders.

Dr. Dale Holloway promotes a program called "Mentoring." In this program a person serves on a staff with another bivocational who is successful and learns how to serve under him. The established bivocational minister helps the other person find work, find a home, learn how to work in a bivocational setting, and later helps him find a bivocational church of his own. "Mentoring" provides "on-the-job" training for the inexperienced bivocational minister.

Denominational leaders are invaluable in knowing and helping a pastor locate all of the training opportunities available in the area. Other bivocationals can also be of help. Whether bivocational pastors train formally in a school setting or informally at home, they must train themselves as completely as possible.

Training for the Secular Work

Training for the secular work will probably take various forms. Persons who have time and opportunity to do so can train for their secular vocation in college and their church vocation in seminary. If they already have seminary training and need a secular vocation in order to move into bivocationalism, they can consider returning to college or a trade school in order to acquire a secular skill. If formal education seems to be out of the question, they can train themselves or serve as an apprentice in some secular vocation into which they can move as soon as they are prepared.

If you are a minister who is planning training for the secular vocation in bivocationalism, you should consider several important matters that will make the secular training more beneficial. First, survey the job market. What jobs or skills are needed in the general area where you plan to serve as a bivocational? The job market in "Silicone Valley" in California, for example, might be different from the job market in one of the rural areas in the deep South. As a prospective bivocational minister, you probably have some general idea where the Lord wants you to serve. Preparation for secular work in that particular area would be a wise plan to follow.

Of course, some vocations are found almost anywhere. A druggist, a lawyer, a teacher, or a social worker might not have to consider the job market as closely for a particular geographic area. Your denominational leaders usually have information or they can get information concerning available secular jobs for particular areas of the country. These leaders can save you from wasted time preparing for a job that isn't available in many places.

A second matter to consider is the nature of the secular vocation. Consider a vocation that is both marketable and portable. Could you find employment in your secular vocation just about anywhere God might lead you to serve? Is your secular vocation portable so that you can move to other churches as God might direct? Many career military people have served as ministers of the gospel. They have often had some input into organizing or serving churches in the places where the government stationed them. They have often decided upon the place of the new assignment in light of the opportunities to be bivocational ministers.

A few bivocational ministers make their secular vocation a management position with a company maintaining plants all over the country. This fact opens up to them the potential of serving bivocational churches wherever the company sends them. Sometimes they are able to request an area where they know bivocational ministries are needed.

A third consideration is the need to evaluate your skills. Bivocationals are divided on their opinions as to what kind of secular vocation to pursue. Some contend for a people-oriented secular vocation, such as that of a teacher, a social workers, or a counselor. The advantage is found in the fact that many ministers score highly in people-oriented vocations. Therefore, the minister would do well with such a secular vocation.

Other bivocationals warn against having two people-oriented vocations. The church work is people oriented. If the secular job is also, the minister might face the danger of burnout. Nonpeople-oriented secular vocations, such as Paul's tentmaking, offer a relief and change from the drain of people and their needs. Some personalities might do much better if the two vocations are different.

How could a bivocational minister find out what kind of secular vocation to pursue? Skills and vocational aptitudes can be evaluated in many ways. Vocational training schools and employment agencies can be found in most areas. They offer vocational aptitude tests that help a person discover his aptitude for secular vocations. These materials can be helpful in deciding on a job. Some ministers have already had these tests and know the findings.

Colleges also offer help in discovering which vocation would probably be most suitable. Many seminarians have gone through these procedures and have the information available to use.

Denominations also have counseling available through seminary counselors or other denominations leaders who can help you discover your natural aptitudes for a secular vocation. These counselors can counsel with you and offer you their resources for choosing a secular career. Many employment agencies also offer testing to determine apptitude talents.

Some ministers who are open to bivocational ministries are those who already have secular interests which they find exciting to pursue. These natural interests can be checked with the available job openings in the area where the bivocational ministry will be done.

Being self-employed is also an option for some bivocationals. They inherit or organize a business which can make them a living and in which they can be their own boss. This has advantages for scheduling and being available for crises which occur on the church field.

A fourth consideration is the training opportunities and advancement possibilities in the secular vocation. Many bivocationals today have had to work at a secular job while serving the church in order to support the family. These men took whatever job was available. Some jobs are satisfying, and some are not. Many men are to be highly commended for working at unfulfilling secular jobs day after day in order to serve their churches and support their families adequately.

However, a younger minister has the opportunity to make some choices concerning a secular vocation if he plans early enough. He should choose a career that offers a fulfilling work with continued training and advancement possibilities. A bivocational is not required to have a boring secular job. He can have one in which he finds personal challenge and fulfillment. He should feel that he is serving God through the secular vocation as well as through the church ministry.

Training for the Church Work

Training for the church work is usually through formal education, such as seminary. But in many denominations the largest percentage of its ministers have been unable to attend seminary. These people are doing great work because they have trained themselves through experience and informal opportunities of personal study. Many kinds of opportunities are available for ministers in any kind of situation.

Even among those who attended seminary, many bivocationals who are serving churches today did not know they would be in this kind of ministry when they attended seminary. Probably most of them prepared for ministry in a full-time pastorate. For whatever reasons, they serve today in a dual-role capacity.

Some bivocational ministers were asked about their perceptions of their strengths and weaknesses. A group of Alabama Southern Baptist bivocational pastors gave the following list of areas in which they felt reasonably knowledgeable and capable:

1. Preaching,
2. Relations with deacons and church members,
3. Relations with other staff members, usually volunteer people,
4. Efficient use of building space, and
5. Relationship to associational program.[3]

These findings suggest that college, seminary, and secular work experiences had adequately prepared them for their church work in these areas.

These same ninety-five bivocational pastors also listed ten needs that they felt in their church work. Some categories had more than one item that received the same number of votes. Those top ten categories of needs and the number of bivocationals who expressed needs in each category are:

1. Christian Social Ministries, 68;
   Evaluating community needs, 68;
2. Skill in counseling, 67;
   Leadership training, 67;
3. Knowledge of other faiths, 65;
   Mission outreach, 65;
   Leadership enlistment, 65;
4. Methods of evangelism, 64;
   Relationship to denominational agencies, 64;
5. Relationship to the Home Mission Board, 61;

Evaluating church needs, 61;
6. Time management, 60;
7. Program planning 59;
8. Relationship to state program, 58;
9. Religious education, 57; and
10. Developing efficient church organizational structures, 55.[4]

These findings suggest areas where students planning on a bivocational ministry need to give particular attention in their training for church ministry if they plan to go to seminary. If seminary is not a possibility, a minister will probably want to seek informal training in these areas and will watch for such training opportunities.

Another group of about three hundred Southern Baptist bivocational pastors was surveyed in 1977. These men were asked to indicate how they felt about their skills in certain areas. The findings are similiar to the Alabama survey. They ranked the areas from most comfortable to least comfortable: (1) Getting along with people; (2) Visiting the sick; (3) Preaching; (4) Witnessing; (5) Sermon preparation; (6) Counseling.[5]

This survey suggests that students planning for a bivocational ministry should give more attention in their training and preparation for the ministry in the areas of counseling, sermon preparation, witnessing, and preaching in that order.

Basic ministerial education is required of all pastors in most denominations. Where this requirement exists, the student training for bivocationalism will receive his basic ministerial training in college and/or seminary. He will receive the basic training deemed necessary for ordination in the church or denomination.

Some denominations encourage but do not require a basic ministerial education for its ministers. The Southern Baptist Convention is one of these denominations. A survey was made in 1983 of the educational attainments of 16,560 Southern Baptist pastors. The survey showed that among these pastors, 43.2 percent completed their basic seminary ministerial training. Among those who were full-time pastors, 54.4 percent completed seminary. Among the bivocational pastors, 15.4 percent completed seminary.[6] Figures for the total number of SBC pastors were not available. Jack Washington, who made this study, reported that among those surveyed, "Approximately 40 percent of BV [bivocational] pastors have at most a high school education."[7]

Several factors explain why many bivocationals do not have a basic ministerial education. The denomination and the churches probably recommend and prefer seminary training but do not require it for ordination or a call to be pastor. Therefore, one can serve a church as pastor without any required educational attainments.

Many bivocational pastors were called to preach later in life. They felt unable to attain a college and seminary education due to age and family responsibilities. These men became available as pastors and were called by churches to begin serving as pastors. Many have natural abilities, were already active as laymen in strong churches, and thus had received on-the-job training in their home churches. Therefore, they are doing a good job in their churches with the abilities they have. Their attitude toward training is reflected in some advice given by the Reverend Jonah Parker whose ministry is presented in chapter 5. Parker said, "Get all the educational and training possible. Many of us did not have this opportunity; therefore, we do the best we know and depend on God for the rest."

No doubt a few pastors, both nonbivocational and bivocational, do not believe in formal education. These pastors shun education for reasons they feel are biblical and preferable. Elements of antieducation are still found among churches and pastors today. And it is their prerogative to believe and practice what they believe to be true. But most bivocationals who do not have much formal education have lacked opportunity to get it.

Some seminaries offer a basic seminary education to ministers who are not college graduates. The seminaries which are in the Southern Baptist Convention are examples. In 1976 the Southern Baptist Convention asked its six seminaries to provide basic ministerial training for those Baptist ministers who do not have college education. At New Orleans Baptist Theological Seminary, the School of Christian Training was reactivated to meet this need. A two-year program of basic ministerial education is offered to anyone twenty-five years of age or older who has a high school diploma. This theological training is offered on the seminary campus in New Orleans and also in several centers in other states in the South. Therefore, a person who is called to preach later in life and who feels that he can't spend four years in college and three years in a seminary before becoming a pastor can obtain a basic theological education in preparation for ministry. Many other seminaries offer the same type of education.

What specific areas of study should a student planning a bivocational ministry consider while receiving his ministerial training? Here are several suggestions. First, the student should work through the theology and philosophy of bivocationalism. Who is the bivocational? Are his role and calling legitimate? Can a person serve God full-time in two vocations, one secular and one religious?

No doubt the average seminary curriculum has the full-time, church-supported minister in mind. The bivocational minister will have to do some "translation" as he takes his courses. He needs to enter bivocationalism convinced and comfortable with the uniqueness of bivocational ministry.

Second, the student should work through the theology and philosophy of the role of an equipping ministry. Due to lack of time and pressing needs among the membership of the church, the minister won't have time or opportunity to minister as he would like. Therefore, he must know how to equip his people to minister beside him. He will need to know how to put ten people to work rather than being able to do the work of ten people. An equipping ministry is a must.

Third, he needs to study administration, particularly church administration. Many preachers prefer to preach rather than work at administration. The full-time pastor might have more time to keep the organizations oiled and working smoothly. But the bivocational pastor needs to know how to get the most accomplished in the shortest period of time. Administration is a must.

Fourth, he needs to study evangelism, missions, and ministry. Thirty to forty hours per week will be spent out in the world on the secular job. By way of contrast, a full-time pastor can spend twenty to thirty hours per week isolated from the world in his study, his office, attending church committee meetings, or being in other religious functions. As salt and light in the world, the bivocational minister should face how he will evangelize and minister for Christ in his secular vocation, as well as in his position as a leader of a church.

Fifth, he needs to be ecumenical in scope while being personally committed to his own church doctrines. The two are not incompatible. Can he be "all things to all men" in order to be able to bear an effective witness to some? He should already know what most people believe or don't believe. Then he can know how to relate positively and helpfully to others on the secular job.

Sixth, he needs to study and practice the strongest family principles possible. He will not have the inclination to make his secular vocation the center of his life. God has called him to preach. He will not have time to make the church the center of his life. He can give only twenty to thirty hours per week to the church. His family can be the focus and center of stability for him. The husband-wife, parent-child relationships can be the constant or basic relationship while he works first at one place and then the other. He won't have an opportunity to cultivate many close relationships with other ministers due to this schedule. The home can be even more significant to the bivocational.

Other suggestions have been offered to the seminary student who is preparing for a bivocational ministry. Dr. Karl Reko urges the student to be involved in as much fieldwork as possible in seminary for the personal, practical experience gained. He suggests participation in an internship if at all possible. As much skill assessment and vocational analysis as possible will be helpful in determining the secular vocation. He also urges that the bivocational learn and be able to use the goal-setting process of planning. He further suggests that one get experiences in community politics and social concerns and become acquainted with active bivocationals already on the field. He concludes, "If potential worker-priests should experience any divergent training, it should be in the area of fieldwork, internship and guidance in employment while at seminary."[8]

Continuing Education

A minister's education is never completed. Business and professional groups want their members to continue to grow. Adult education is a growing field in education today. The bivocational minister has never had more opportunities to continue his education than he does today.

He needs to grow vocationally in his secular field. Being an "example of the believer" isn't applicable just to working in a church. God wants us to become our best in all areas.

Most all secular vocations have training opportunities. Some companies pay for further education received. Colleges, universities, and trade schools are making educational opportunities more readily available. Courses are taught at night, at the noon hour in locations away from the campus and nearer the students, on Saturdays, and throughout the summer. Many will not even need to go to the college campus to take these courses.

Some businesses and firms offer and even require continued training. Depending upon the business, any training opportunities will help the employee do a better job. There is also a spillover into the work of the church. For example, a course on selling or on building customer relationships designed for the company's employees will also benefit the bivocational pastor in church work. Continuing education is a response to the stewardship of one's talents and opportunities.

The minister also wants to continue growing in his vocation as a minister in the church. Things change. The minister changes as he passes through the various stages of life. The church changes as it meets new challenges, and it needs new approaches. The community often changes, as it is affected by the economic and sociological changes brought on by either growing, declining, or static population figures. A seminary education tries to be timeless, but it is inevitably dated. Therefore, the minister must continue to train himself for effective service.

Each denomination is committed to continuing ministerial education in a variety of ways. National, state, and local training facilities are available for conferences, seminars, and week-long classes in a variety of subjects. Correspondence courses are available. Books can be checked out from most local college, seminary, or universal libraries. Tapes and cassettes, both audio and video, which have study materials in most areas of church work are becoming more available. Cable television is opening home study opportunities for everything from foreign language courses to Bible study courses. Denominations are producing training cassettes to be aired over local cable television channels. Some churches are purchasing equipment to be able to receive these training program live in their own churches.

Many seminaries are enlarging their curriculum offerings through their continuing education programs. Ministers can attend courses either on campus or at some local center where courses are offered at a time convenient and nearer to the pastor on the field. Many opportunities for training are one day, weekend, or week-long seminars. Credit can also be obtained for many of these continuing education courses. Your denominational leaders can help you discover what is available to you in your area.

Most denominations will also offer seminars and training opportunities in most every area of church life through either state or associational training meetings. In my own denomination, most ministers can receive valuable training by attending association, regional, or state training opportunities offered throughout the year. One main obstacle at this point is the time such meetings are scheduled. Sometimes these training events are not offered when the bivocational is available. Church leaders are becoming much more aware of this need and are seeking ways to schedule events when the bivocational is available.

In conclusion, the dual-role minister needs to begin training himself specifically for a bivocational ministry as early as possible. He needs training both in his secular work and in his church work. This dual training needs to continue. The trend is for more opportunities for continuing education to become available as the church learns how to utilize the technology of the day. Opportunities for training in the home are already available through the use of computers, home satellite dishes, and video recorders. The future is exciting in potential.

If you are a bivocational minister, where are you in terms of your professional growth in your secular work and in your church work? Do you have long-range goals in each area? You might work up some goals in both areas of your work. Then, you could begin to look to see what training opportunities you can find to help you reach these goals.

Notes

1. H. Karl Reko, "Determinative Factors in the Ability of Christ Seminary—Seminex Graduates to Conduct Worker-Priest Ministries in the United States." An unpublished D.Minn. thesis of the Eden Theological Seminary, St. Louis, Mo., 1980, p. 52.

2. Those seminaries were Boston School of Theology, Princeton Theological Seminary, Louisville Theological Seminary, Pittsburgh Theological Seminary, Midwestern Baptist Theological Seminary,

New Brunswich Theological Seminary, Saint Meinrad School of Theology, and Lexington Theological Seminary.

3. J. T. Burdine, Jr., "Alabama Bivocational Pastors Survey Summary," 1 October 1980. An unpublished report, p. 1.

4. Ibid., pp. 1-2.

5. Lewis Wingo, "The Needs of Bi-Vocational Pastors," *The Quarterly Review* (April-May-June 1979): 44-45.

6. Jack L. Washington, "Study of Bivocational Pastors and Churches in the SBC, 1983," SBC Home Mission Board, Atlanta, Ga. (September 1984): 34.

7. Ibid., p. 30.

8. Reko, p. 146.

10

Preparing the People

A church needs to make preparations if it decides to become a bivocational church. A smooth transition needs to be made. Meaningful and acceptable relationships need to be established and maintained between the church membership and the minister.

Many small churches have always had dual-role ministers. They have never had ministers who were fully supported financially by their church and living on the field in their midst. These churches need to feel good about their bivocational status because it is legitimate and important.

Reasons Churches Are Bivocational

One way a church can prepare itself for a bivocational pastor is to realize that many other churches are also bivocational. These churches become bivocational for at least one or more of five reasons. Economics is an underlying factor but not the only consideration.

First, many new churches are bivocational. They are small in membership and are unable to support a minister financially in a full-time relationships. Whereas denominations supplement the minister's salary in some new churches, they also promote bivocationalism as a way to organize and serve new churches.

Many new churches are strong and are growing at a rate faster than other bivocational churches. A 1983 study done in the Southern Baptist Convention revealed the strength of these new bivocational churches.[1] Southern Baptists reported 312 new bivocational churches organized between 1980 and 1983. Half of them are located in open country, villages, or small towns. Twenty-seven are in large cities. These bivo- cational churches are more effective in some areas of minis- try than older bivocational churches or other full-time churches. For example, Jack Washington found in this sur- vey that new, rural bivocational churches had a greater rate of baptisms per 100 resident members (11.8 baptisms) than did older bivocational churches (4.3 baptisms). The rate was also higher than the entire Convention (3.9 baptisms per 100 resident members). The rate of additions to the churches by other methods was also higher. The same higher rate was found in Sunday School enrollment, Church Training enroll- ment, and mission organizational enrollment. Per capita giv- ing was higher in the new rural churches than in other rural bivocational churches, but somewhat lower than in the en- tire Convention. These findings led Washington to conclude, "On the whole newer small rural BV churches are stronger than older BV churches."[2]

A second reason many churches are bivocational is their size. Some have been organized, functioning, stable church- es for years. Yet, these churches are too few in membership to support the ministry of a full-time pastor. Lyle Schaller reported that one half of all Protestant congregations aver- age less than seventy-five people attending the principal worship service each week.[3] The normal-size Protestant con- gregation on the North American continent has closer to forty people at worship on a typical Sunday morning.[4]

A number of these churches do support full-time pastors. These churches are unusually strong financially with few outstanding debts. Many own a debt-free church building and a debt-free pastor's home. Therefore, up to 50 percent of their budgets can be used for pastoral salary.

But most of the small churches require either denomina- tional supplement for their ministers or bivocational pastors. Almost 90 percent of all bivocational churches in the Southern Baptist Convention have a membership of less than three hundred.[5]

A third reason some churches are bivocational is the fact that they are declining in membership and are often located in declining neighborhoods. It is not at all uncommon to find a church building in the open country, in a village, a small town, or in a section of a city that can seat five hundred people, but the membership is down to an attendance of two hundred. Upkeep on the buildings, utility costs, and dwindling income have been the factors that require the church to seek a bivocational pastor or a bivocational staff member instead of full-time ministers.

These churches need much help in moving from a full-time minister to a bivocational minister without feeling defeated and hopeless. These churches need not feel like they are going backward. Communities and churches change. Growing communities tend to have growing churches. Declining communities tend to have churches whose memberships are either stable or declining. If a church is God's people on mission for Him in a particular community, the church is responsible for whatever community it is in. That church can be just as faithful and effective with the potential it has in a declining neighborhood with smaller numbers as it was once in a growing neighborhood with larger numbers. Bivocational churches are not second-class, ineffective churches. They do better in some areas of church life than their full-time counterparts.

A fourth reason for bivocationalism in some churches is the desire of these churches to utilize a bivocational staff. By being bivocational, the church can utilize the services of more staff members for specialized leadership of the church program.

The Brookstown Baptist Church of Baton Rouge, Louisiana, had a bivocational church staff under the leadership of bivocational pastor Stafford Rogers. Five associates handled their assigned functions during their twenty-hour workweek. They covered visitation and pastoral care, music and youth, outreach and children's church, religious education, and new ministries.[6]

Clark Street Baptist Church of Johnson City, Tennessee, had three bivocational staff members and one full-time church secretary. The pastor was also in the insurance business. The minister of music was with the United States Postal Service. The associate pastor was a Pepsi-Cola operations manager. This church averaged 130 in Sunday School.

A fifth reason some churches are bivocational is the result of a conscious choice to be bivocational rather than full-time, even though being full-time is possible. Some of these churches are large, and some are small.

The Clifton Baptist Church of Franklinton, Louisiana, made such a choice. During a period of its ministry, the church decided not to call a full-time pastor as they had previously. Rather, they chose to call a bivocational pastor to serve them in a ministry of twenty-five to thirty hours per week. This enabled the church also to call a student youth minister who was attending the nearby seminary to serve them on the weekends. The church was able to increase its local missions giving from 2 percent to 4 percent and its national missions giving from 8 percent to 12 percent. A scholarship fund for college students was also initiated. The church felt that a bivocational pastor could serve them effectively and being a bivocational church would enable them to do some extra things without making much more demands on the budget.

These are several of the reasons churches are bivocational. Bivocational status often changes, even from one pastor to the next one. But it is not necessarily a step backward to adopt a dual-role ministry as the best approach to pastoral leadership at a particular time. The next pastoral change might go in a different direction.

Preparing the Church

Bivocationalism is a new concept to some church leaders, although it goes all the way back to the Bible. Therefore, time spent preparing the church for this type of pastoral leadership will be time well spent.

Most churches enter a bivocational relationship with their minister because of economic necessity. Karl Reko, in a doctor of ministry project study of dual-role pastorates, said, "Every congregational leader interviewed said his/her parish called a worker-priest because that was the only way they could have their own pastor . . . . the common motive was financial necessity."[7] Therefore, the congregation is prone to believe that this is "all we can do," and that it is second-best and not first-class. The assumption is that the ideal, the preferred, the best situation in all churches is a full-time pastor living on the field, fully supported financially by the church.

But that assumption doesn't deal realistically with the facts. If half of the Protestant churches have forty or less in worship each Sunday, full-time financial support of all of their pastoral staffs just isn't possible. Are these small churches aberrations of real churches? Is it realistic, not to mention Christian, to expect churches to be able to support their ministries full-time financially when that possibility is out of the question? Don't these facts suggest that some other arrangements will be the norm for many small churches? Some churches will be able to support their ministers full-time. And both kinds of churches will be normal, bona fide, legitimate, first-class churches with each doing its best with what it has.

As churches work through the philosophy of bivocationalism, they are also enlightened and encouraged to find that this type of ministry is as old as the Old and New Testaments. It has biblical precedents. Also, it is found throughout history as the practice in all kinds of religious communions. In fact, full-time ministers supported by their churches may be the new kid on the block historically. And churches need to know that bivocational pastorates often do better than their full-time counterparts. These facts will challenge churches to be open to the will of God concerning bivocationalism.

A church that is considering entering a bivocational relationship with a minister might work through a form like the one entitled "Church Desiring a Bivocational Pastor Information Form" found in the Appendix of this book. This form leads the church to consider such matters as why it is becoming bivocational, what needs the church has at the present time, what such a minister would be asked to do in the church, and what financial arrangements the church could make with the minister. Such a form is a good piece of information to share with a prospective or a new bivocational minister.

There is also a form in the Appendix that is entitled "Prospective Bivocational Pastor Information Form." This is a good way for a church to gather some valuable information on a prospective pastor. The form calls for information about former church experiences, secular work experiences, attitudes toward bivocational ministry, needs in such areas as finances and help in seeking a secular job, and some names of people who would serve as references who know the minister and his work.

These two forms are used in the Southern Baptist Convention by churches and pastors who are involved in the newer areas of the Convention. But the information called for would help any church or pastor. The forms could be adapted to reflect more accurately a particular church or denomination.

Another important consideration in preparing the church is that of mutually agreeing upon the expectations that the church and the bivocational pastor have concerning each other. Dr. Reko also found in his study that this consideration was overlooked at great expense later on: "The absence of an initial contract mutually arrived at has plagued the ministry of many worker-priests and the groups served .... The mutuality of the contract is more important than the contract itself."[8]

J. T. Burdine and Dale Holloway of the Southern Baptist Convention have used what Burdine calls a "Covenant for Ministry."[9] (See Appendix for a copy of this convenant.) In this covenant, the prospective bivocational minister and the church leadership look at twenty-three ministries which are needed in most churches. The minister and the church leaders together arrive at the total number of hours per week that should be given to each ministry. The bivocational pastor states the number of hours he feels he can give to each ministry. Then, the church members can see the number of hours per week they will need to give if the ministry is sufficiently covered. Such a procedure forces both the bivocational pastor and the church members to see that the pastor will not be able to do all the work himself. The church will have to assume more responsibility in order for the ministries to be accomplished. The pastor will need to be more of an overseer and an equipper, helping the church members become equipped for ministry. Together they form the people of God and a team committed to ministry in their community and church.

In the CODE Project in New York, the participants discovered some helpful guidelines for congregations to follow before calling their first dual-role minister.

1. List functions to be accomplished and by whom.
2. Estimate time requirements for each function.
3. Establish priorities which will be pursued first.
4. Realign functions to cover the new relationships that will exist under bivocationalism.
5. Develop a clear job description and schedule that is acceptable to the church and the minister.
6. Establish periodic reviews in order the review the past and plan together for the future.[10]

Working Together as Pastor and People

Many bivocational pastorates are finding the requirements of such a ministry both challenging and satisfying. The Reverend Gideon Von Galambos of the CODE Project in New York said, "Dual-Role pastors represent the rebirth of New Testament partnerships."[11] Several factors are evident in this phenomenon.

First, churches, not just pastors, serve Christ in a community. Churches do not pay the preacher to do the work of the church for them. Churches call pastors to lead them in serving the Lord and the community in their area.

Second, all believers are ministers. The terms *lay* and *clergy* are used to distinguish nonordained and ordained church workers. But, basically, all believers are called to minister. Therefore, God's work can't be accomplished just by the professional clergy in the churches. All of God's people are responsible for the work of the ministry (Eph. 4:12).

Third, all believers are given gifts by the Holy Spirit to exercise in the body of Christ (Rom. 12; 1 Cor. 12—14). Believers do not have the same gifts. All Holy Spirit-given gifts are needed. Therefore, one person, even the pastor, could not do the work of all their gifts even if he wanted to. All believers have their own essential work that God wants them to do.

Fourth, Paul seems to have taught that God gives leaders like "pastors" in order to equip and lead the believers in a church to do their ministries (Eph. 4:11-12). This gift of pastor is a "gift to the gifts" which are found among the believers in the church. The pastor is to equip them to find, develop, and execute their ministries. The pastor has his function in the church; the believers have their functions. Together, they form the people of God under Christ, their Lord, through the power of the indwelling Holy Spirit to labor together in the work of the kingdom.

These factors fit the possibilities offered in bivocationalism. An Episcopal Church leader observed, "What time the Dual-Role pastor has for the church must be spent in training lay people to do things which in the past were done for them."[12]

In conclusion, the church must be prepared for a bivocational ministry. A church cannot turn to bivocationalism as a cop-out for unwillingness to be good stewards financially. God expects believers to be all that they are capable of becoming. But for many churches, the ability to support a pastor with all of his financial needs will not be possible. To these churches bivocationalism becomes a real option. When churches and pastors face bivocationalism, understand its philosophy and unique characteristics, and agree upon a plan of ministry together, these churces have a chance to have a satisfactory and fulfilling ministry in bivocationalism.

The CODE Project discovered seven reasons churches see bivocationalism as a valid, emerging alternative for pastoral ministry:[13]

1. *Initiative.* Churches can take the initiative and choose bivocationalism instead of feeling thrust into it.

2. *Sense of Mission.* All the members can feel a sense of personal responsibility for the work of the church since the pastor's time with them is limited.

3. *Development.* Small churches can work on their own resources and potentials instead of being jealous for the resources and potentials of larger churches.

4. *Evaluation.* The church must evaluate its ministry, its resources, and its possibilities. This procedure often brings new life to the people.

5. *Equality.* "D-R [Dual-Role] lifts all participants to the rank of discipleship with room to grow."[14]

6. *Programming.* New forms of ministry and new people in ministry often come from the bivocational relationship.

7. *Diversity.* Through bivocationalism churches can have a pastor. In bivocationalism churches can build new relationships and assume new responsibilities unknown in the past.

Notes

1. See Jack L. Washington, "Study of Bivocational Pastors and Churches in the Southern Baptist Convention, 1983," SBC Home Mission Board, Atlanta, Ga. (September 1984):18ff.

2. Ibid., p. 20.

3. Lyle E. Schaller, *The Small Church IS Different* (Nashville: Abingdon Press, 1982), p. 11.

4. Ibid., p. 9.

5. Washington, p. 16.

6. Thurman Allred, "A Bivocational Church Staff?" *Church Administration* (January 1981): 33-34.

7. H. Karl Reko, "Determinative Factors in the Ability of Chirst Seminary—Seminex Graduates to Conduct Worker-Priest Ministries in the United States." An unpublished D.Min. thesis of the Eden Theological Seminary, St. Louis, Mo. (1980): 132.

8. Ibid., p. 133.

9. J. T. Burdine, Jr., "Covenant for Ministry," *The Tentmaker's Journal* (March-June 1980): 6.

10. Clergy Occupational Development and Employment Project, *Dual-Role Pastorates* (Rochester: Clergy Occupational and Employment Project, 1978), p. 35.

11. Ibid., p. 33.

12. Ibid.

13. Ibid., pp. 34-35.

14. Ibid., p. 34.

Locating the Partners

The bivocational pastor needs all the assistance he can get. The bivocational church also needs to know the sources of help available to it throughout the week. This chapter suggests some sources of help which are available to most bivocational clergy and churches today.

James Lowery said, "Parish pastors look for support above, below, behind, to the left, and to the right."[1] The support sought from above is that of denominational leaders, such as the bishop, district leaders, and other various denominational agencies. The support needed from below is the congregation in the church. The wife and home provide the support from behind. The support from the left comes from other professions in a community, such as psychiatrists, marriage counselors, and other ministry services. Finally, the support from the right is peer support, coming from the support from fellow clergymen who accept and encourage the bivocational.

What kind of help is available today for bivocational pastors and churches? There is help from the secular world and there is help from the church world.

Partners from the Secular Field

Most pastors are taught to be all things to all people. In the past many of them were. They were the best educated people of their communities and could answer many questions for their people. They frequently knew more about most things either through training or experience than the average person knew. Therefore, the minister who was present on the church field was a source of help for many people in many areas.

He could often give good counsel to his people on most any problem they had. He either knew or could readily find the answers to various legal questions. He probably even passed on medical remedies or at least directed people to the proper medical personnel who could provide answers. He was available for counsel, for transportation, and for assistance throughout the week to the members of his community.

The bivocational isn't available for that kind of relationship to his people. He is with them only twenty-five to thirty hours per week. Yet people continue to have needs that require assistance from someone. The pastor and the people need to know what partners are available for assistance from the secular field.

First, many counseling services are available. Most communities either have a mental health facility or one is nearby. These facilities are organized and dedicated to the mental health of the community. The members of a bivocational church might not have their pastor available to them day and night. Therefore, the church should be alerted to the presence and location of counseling services which will be available to the people when needed.

Most communities today have all types of professional counselors. There is less stigma today against seeking professional counseling. There are more counselors in specialized fields, such as family, children, and drugs, that ever before. Local schools and colleges frequently have counselors to whom church members can turn for help. The pastor and church leaders can educate the members concerning these services. Therefore, the church will not feel that it is neglected in this area.

Second, most communities have legal services available, or these legal services are located within an easy driving distance. Pastors and long-established church leaders know lawyers who are available in the community and who have good reputations. Most full-time pastors cultivate the friendship of a lawyer who can be contacted for some general advice about which direction to tell a church member to go seeking legal help. A quick call can provide the answer about what the first step should be. The church people can be alerted to who is available for the many questions a full-time pastor is asked concerning legal matters. Information is often needed before action is taken. Most communities have resources, but these resources need to be identified and publicized.

Third, all communities have medical services available. These services include a diagnosis and treatment, as well as preventive medicine. A full-time pastor works with many people throughout the year as they consider medical treatment, locate medical help, receive the treatment, and then recuperate from it all physically, emotionally, and financially. A bivocational pastor wants that same help available for his church people. Yet, he isn't there to offer it throughout the week. He needs to locate and educate his congregation about those who are available to help.

Much is being said today about a holistic approach to ministry. For example, medical people might emphasize medicine, physical exercise, and a meaningful religious faith as the prescription for an illness. Our age of specialization has fragmented the individual. But the emphasis is returning to that of seeing a person simultaneously as physical, mental, emotional, and spiritual. He needs to be treated holistically, not just specifically.

This holistic approach is needed in the church also. Church members have needs other than spiritual needs. The pastor sees himself as a member of a team, who along with mental health, legal, medical, and educational people serve those particular church members. Each has an area of primary interest, but none can do it all. Therefore, all are in partnership, serving the community. The bivocational pastor finds his hope here. He isn't available to his people as much as he would like to be. Even if he were, he couldn't meet all of their needs alone. So he locates his partners and educates his people to the existence of those available to help them in the matter of daily living.

Partners from the Religious Field

A bivocational minister can also find sources of help in his church ministry from a number of religious organizations. These organizations provide a variety of assistance.

THE ASSOCIATION

Many churches are organized together into associations. These local associations, which often cover a city or a county, assist the local churches and provide a channel of ministries needed in the area. The local association should be considered a partner to the bivocational minister.

Many associations provide training opportunities which are conducted near the churches. These training opportunities are planned for all of the workers in a local church organization. For example, Sunday School workers are offered training in teaching methods for their age groups and in administrative procedures for organizing and directing their classes and departments. Since the bivocational pastor can't be available to his church to do this training himself, he can use the training opportunities offered by his association and see that his church leaders take advantage of this training.

Some associations offer fellowship and ministry opportunities to certain age groups in the churches. Many associations have organized youth programs, singles ministries, senior adult ministries, and both women and men's ministries. A bivocational minister probably finds his congregation too small for an active ministry just for his own church in each of these areas. However, he can lead his people to participate in these fellowship and ministry organizations on the associational level. In that way, his people can benefit as well as contribute to areas of ministry organized specifically for their own particular group.

A bivocational pastor can also help some of his people

find opportunities for enlarged ministries through the local association. These association needs volunteer workers in all of its organizations and ministries just like the church does. These volunteer workers must come from the local churches. An alert bivocational pastor can help some of his members to become available for places of service in the association. Such enlarged ministries will help the church member grow and make a contribution outside of his church as well as within his church. Small churches have many qualified workers who would make a great contribution to their local association. But these church members need to be enlisted and encouraged in this matter by their pastor.

Not only do churches help out in the associational programs but the association can help the local church in various specific ways other than training opportunities as well. When Hoyle Allred was director of missions in Gastonia, North Carolina, he led his associational forces to help bivocational pastors do their work in a number of ways.[2] A bivocational pastor who also was an insurance agent wanted to take a religious survey of his church field but had inadequate time or personnel to do so. A nearby church was enlisted by the director of missions to assist the bivocational minister by providing workers and materials. The joint task was accomplished.

Another bivocational pastor needed encouragement and help in attending a special week-long retreat. Through the association, the director offered him an expense-paid trip to the retreat.

Allred reported some other ways he led his association to assist bivocational pastors.
1. The association helped bivocational churches find bivocational pastors.
2. It provided scholarships to national assemblies for training for some bivocational pastors and their wives.
3. A new bivocational church was offered the use of the associational office as a meeting place until they could provide their own building.

4. Some bivocationals were given educational scholarships to encourage them to complete their education.
5. Meetings were planned with the bivocational's schedule in mind.
6. A seminary extension center was organized and operated in the association where seminary training could be received by ministers desiring it.[3]

Maynard Head wrote of his relationship to the local association through the years. He spoke of the advantages of working in partnerships with the local association. He gave some advice to other bivocational pastors.[4]

First, plan to attend certain associational meetings. Though time won't permit attendance at all of them, some meetings like the pastor's conference or the annual associational meeting are essential.

Second, serve on committees which do not require huge amounts of time. He said, "I have been a bivocational pastor for over ten years and have served as associational stewardship chairman, evangelism chairman, and as a member of the credentials, missions, and resolutions committees."[5]

Third, urge associational leaders to plan some events on Saturdays or during the evenings. This will allow more bivocational pastors and their people to attend. These suggestions came from the benefits Head received for working in the association.

THE STATE CONVENTION

The state convention can be a second partner available to bivocational pastors. Whereas an association is made up of churches in a local area, the state convention covers a larger area than the association but a smaller area than the national convention. The state convention is organized to give leadership and assistance to the denomination's work in a given state or possibly a multiple-state area.

The Reverend Hollis Bryant is a staff member of the Mississippi Baptist Convention. His job assignment includes working with the 454 bivocationals. In an interview with

Bryant, he shared his concern and vision for bivocationalism in his state. He has been planning bivocational events on the state level for the past eight years. He made several observations.

First, the bivocational ministries in the state should be identified and located and a program of ministry planned with them in mind. In the Mississippi, convention 23.3 percent of the churches have bivocational pastors. In one association as many as 40 out of the 50 pastors are bivocational. Bryant plans various programs with these 454 pastors in mind each year.

Second, bivocational ministers should be listened to. Bryant says that he has tried to listen to these pastors as they have shared their gripes, their dreams, their problems, and their needs. Many bivocationals feel they are a neglected and overlooked group of ministers. State leadership can reach many of them by providing a listening ear.

Third, schedule meetings throughout the state for bivocationals and don't cancel them. Often attendance will be small, but those who do attend will benefit.

Fourth, use bivocationals on programs. When full-time pastors of large churches are always the speakers on various programs, bivocational pastors do not feel important or even needed. Bryant seeks to use their talents and give them an opportunity to be heard.

Fifth, give more attention to bivocationalism as part of the answer to reaching people for Christ in areas where there are few or no churches. Bryant sees bivocationalism as part of the solution to three facts present today: (1) There are areas of the nation and world where there is little or no Christian witness; (2) there is an oversupply of ministers in areas like the deep South; and (3) there is God's command to win the lost and build churches. Even without adequate financial resources in the churches, modern-day tentmaking is a viable use of these three facts.

Other state conventions are giving more attention to bivocationalism today than they did in the past. So many leaders believe that it is the wave of the future. A 1983 survey in the Arkansas Baptist Convention revealed the existence of 352 bivocational pastors, which was 27.8 percent of all churches in that state convention. The convention's state paper, *Arkansas Baptist Newsmagazine,* highlighted the ministry of bivocationalism throughout 1985 by publishing articles of information, encouragement, and case history studies of bivocational ministers in the state. This decision enhanced bivocationalism. Bivocational pastors received attention they deserve and need. Bivocational churches felt better about themselves with this kind of publicity. State conventions can be helpful partners with their bivocational ministers.

THE NATIONAL CONVENTION

A national convention can also be a partner to the bivocational pastor and church. National conventions are giving greater attention today to dual-role ministries than they did in the past.

Some churches or national conventions have been unable to recognize or promote dual-role ministries due to their organization and requirements for ordination and ministerial ministries. James L. Lowery pointed out some of the relationships that have existed in the past between national church organizations and dual-role ministries. He said that the hierarchy or the national organizations have looked upon self-supporting priesthoods in three ways:

1. This kind of ministry is underground, secret, or irregular and, therefore, not officially recognized as a legitimate kind of ministry.
2. Bivocationalism may be above ground but unofficial. It exists, but it is not sanctioned nor preferred.
3. This ministry exists, is needed, and has been made official.[6]

During this same time, the dual-role ministers have looked on their hierarchy in several ways:

1. Some agree that bivocationalism isn't a good idea and are marking time until a full-time pastorate opens.
2. Others have worked both secretly and openly to change the status of their ministry. They have called for equal recognition.
3. Some bivocationals are hostile to the hierarchy and have written them off, seeing no need for anything but the local church.
4. Some just ignore the hierarchy, having little time for church matters anyway and not wanting to spend any of it outside their churches.[7]

It seems fair to include another category of those bivocationals who are committed to all phases of their denominational work and who are participating actively and helpfully as time permits.

The CODE Project in 1975-1978 illustrated the complexities of the relationships and attitudes toward dual-role pastorates found in various denominations. Those seven judicatories representing four denominations[8] changed their views from one of caution to one of optimism concerning the possibilities of dual-role ministries.[9] The national offices of several denominations have expressed interest in the CODE Project and its findings. The participants in the project concluded with this observation: *"If Dual-Role ministries is to become something more than a passing experiment,* positive provision for it must be incorporated into the judicatory system."[10]

An example of what some national conventions are doing in the area of bivocationalism is found in the Southern Baptist Convention. The Sunday School Board has an employee who works with bivocational ministries. The Home Mission Board has a bivocational consultant. Many Baptist state conventions have someone designated in the state organizations to give leadership in bivocational ministries. Courses are offered on the bivocational minister in many Baptist seminaries. Nationwide bivocational conferences are conducted from time to time. More materials are being prepared with the small church in mind.

Some bivocational ministers are finding encouragement and support from area-wide bivocational fellowships. An example of such a group is the Fellowship of Bivocational Ministers among Southern Baptist bivocational ministers in Florida. Organized in 1984 as the first bivocational fellowship in the Southern Baptist Convention, the fellowship is "to provide conferences, programs, retreats, a newsletter and to enhance the image and ministry of all bivocational ministers."[11] The Florida Baptist Convention and the Home Mission Board are vitally involved in this ministry.

In summary, many partners are available. These partners are not always known or located; however, they are usually there. The bivocational church or bivocational pastor need not feel isolated or alone any longer.

Notes

1. James L. Lowery, Jr., *Peers, Tents, and Owls* (New York: Morehouse-Barlow Co., 1973), p. 5

2. See Hoyle T. Allred, "The Director of Missions and the Bivocational Pastor," *Church Administration* (February 1982): 41-42.

3. Ibid., pp. 41-42.

4. See K. Maynard Head, "The Bivocational and the Association," *Church Administration* (December 1980): 41-42.

5. Ibid., p. 41.

6. Lowery, pp. 97-98.

7. Ibid., p. 27.

8. Those four denominations were United Presbyterian Church in the USA, American Baptist Convention, Protestant Episcopal Church, and United Church of Christ.

9. See James B. Prichard, "Judicatories and Dual-Role," *Dual-Role Pastorates* (Rochester: Clergy Occupational Employment Project, 1978), pp. 26-31.

10. Ibid., p. 27.

11. *Florida Baptist Witness,* 11 December 1986, p. 6.

12

Responding to the Potential

Bivocationalism faces tremendous potential in this last quarter of the twentieth century. This potential is found in the hope it offers to small churches, the strategy it contains in starting new churches here in the United States, and the vehicle it provides for the relatively new area of overseas bivocational missions.

Responding to the Potential of Small Churches

James Lowery of the Episcopal Church verbalized the problem that many small churches face. He wrote, "The size of the local congregation that is the norm is below the level at which there can be a properly supported, ordained, professional staff, and a properly equipped church, parish house, and rectory/parsonage."[1] He suggested three options such churches have: (1) forego building a church edifice and use those finances for the support of a minister and other needs of the church; (2) share a pastor with several other churches in the area, thus making the church require less money for ministerial salary; or (3) call a pastor who earns part or all of his living secularly. Lowery advocated the last option as a viable one for many small churches.

The number of small churches has already been discussed. Some denominations have over 50 percent of their churches being served by a bivocational pastor already. In 1980, J. T. Burdine quoted from an article in *Money* magazine which said:

Inadequate compensation is inevitable with small congregations. At one time it was felt that 200 members were necessary to support a full-time minister. Now, 300-400 are
necessary. Church mergers are increasing and nearly half of
the 365,000 Christian ministers in the United States has a
second occupation.[2]

Phil Rodgerson, director of missions for Virginia Southern
Baptists, in a paper entitled "The Future of the Small Church
in Non-Metropolitan Areas," observed: "It is estimated that
in the decade of the eighties, it will take an average $2 per
member per Sunday with an average Sunday morning worship attendance of 130-145 persons to support a full-time
seminary-trained pastor."[3]

These figures would not hold up in every denomination
and among all churches. But they do indicate that many
small churches are having problems supporting a full-time
minister. The wives of many pastors feel that they have to
work outside the home to help provide an adequate income.
This fact supports the impressions that many churches
would, indeed, have trouble providing the total income that
a minister's family needs. Bivocationalism is an option to
them.

Many small churches have the potential for growth. Some
are finding that under the leadership of a bivocational pastor
they can grow. The larger churches usually lead the way in
total numbers in such areas as budgets, baptisms, and number and cost of buildings. Small churches frequently lead the
way in such things as per capita giving to the budget, baptisms per one hundred members, and percentage of debt-free
budget money available for ministry and missions. Bivocational churches have been found to do better on a percentage
basis reaching more of their membership on a regular basis
and involving them in the various activities of the church.
Strong pastoral leadership is usually found in the small
churches that are growing. Bivocationalism is a way many
of these small churches can have a pastor.

Daryl Heath, a consultant who works with small churches

in the Southern Baptist Convention, wrote recently of the effectiveness of small churches. He identified some of the strengths and reasons for their effectiveness. Some of those factors were:[4]

1. Small churches are important because there are so many of them in our country.
2. Growth can and is taking place in these churches.
3. Many small churches have growth-potential.
4. Small churches are a training ground for future church leaders in all churches.
5. Everybody is somebody in a small church.
6. Communication is necessary and possible in a small church. Most people know what is going on.
7. Many future pastors come from small churches.
8. The pastor has a strong influence among his people.
9. A warm, caring fellowship often results in a higher baptismal ratio per member than is found in larger churches.
10. Many small churches have bivocational pastors who are serving in an effective manner.

Bivocationalism meets the need for trained, capable ministers in small churches. In bivocationalism the church will not be responsible for the total financial support of a pastor. The pastor will not depend completely upon the church as the place for his total ministry and the exercise of his gifts. Both pastor and people find these advantages in a dual-role pastoral relationship. Yet, each church can have its own pastor.

Responding to the Potential of New Work at Home

If a self-supporting minister has a secular vocation that is marketable and portable, he can go many places where there is a need for a minister to begin a new mission and get a church started. This possibility is a vision that many denominational leaders see for starting new work.

The Home Mission Board of the Southern Baptist Convention promotes the starting of new work through the use of bivocational ministers. A promotional piece called *Ministers of the Marketplace* presents the church-starting potential of bivocational pastors.

In this brochure Elaine Furlow says that Southern Baptists desire to begin new missions in many places throughout the United States. One Baptist state leader reported that he had identified "150 sites for new churches . . . but we can't afford to put full-time pastors in each of them."[5] Another state leader knew of fifteen places where bivocational ministers could begin new missions.

Furlow suggested that bivocationalism is an approach that offers an advantage in starting new work other than the financial advantage. She quoted Jack Redford of the SBC Home Mission Board, who was once a schoolteacher/pastor: "A church-planter . . . . desperately needs a sense of identity in the community; being bivocational can give a person a foothold."[6] Many new churches in all denominations trace their roots to the effective groundwork done by a bivocational minister and his family. This is still an effective approach for starting new work today.

Responding to the Potential of Overseas Missions

Bivocationalism in overseas missions is another area of tremendous potential facing the church today. The church has responded in the past by sending self-supporting missionaries to foreign missions. Many are doing the same thing today.

William Carey, called "the Father of Modern Missions," was a bivocational foreign missionary from England to India. During the first five years of missionary service in India, with little or no financial support coming from England, Carey supported himself as superintendent of an indigo factory. Later he supported himself and his two colleagues, Marshman and Ward, through teaching Bengali, Marathi, and Sanskrit in the government-owned Fort William College at Calcutta.[7]

Carey believed in bivocational foreign missions. He once

wrote about bivocationalism: "We have ever held it to be an essential principle in the conduct of missions, that whenever it is practicable, missionaries should support themselves in whole or in part through their own exertions."[8]

J. Christy Wilson, Jr., advocates tentmaking in foreign missions. Wilson's book has the subtitle: "Self-support: An Alternative Model for Worldwide Witness." He stated his purpose in these words: "The purpose of this book is to inspire, inform, encourage, and challenge those whom God is calling to serve as his tentmakers, his self-supporting witnesses around the world."[9]

Wilson presented a brief history of tentmaking in overseas missions.[10] He began with the early Christians in Persia in the fourth and fifth centuries who fled persecution but preached wherever they went, supporting themselves financially. He cited the example of the Roman Catholic Jesuit missionaries in the sixteenth century who supported themselves financially in foreign mission labors through the silk trade. Protestant chaplains of the East India Company, such as the Reverend Henry Martyn of India foreign mission fame, were supported by the company which had employed them as chaplains. The Moravian missionaries were challenged "to shoulder their artisan's tools and follow the Lamb in a mission to the world."[11] These examples indicate that overseas bivocationals have been used in various places throughout history in foreign missions.

Most denominations today can relate their experiences with self-supporting missionaries overseas. Many English-speaking churches have been established in foreign countries by military people, oil people, and other kinds of business employees. These churches serve the English-speaking communities and also reach out in a witness and ministry to the national population of the area. Many churches stand today as a result of the witness of these self-supported "missionaries" who witnessed for Christ while they lived for periods of time in a foreign land.

Most denominations have programs similar to the work of

the Southern Baptist Foreign Mission Board in Richmond, Virginia.[12] The primary emphasis of the Board is on career missionaries: those men and women fully supported by the Board in full-time overseas missions. Over three thousand of these men and women were serving overseas in 1987. In addition to these, over five thousand persons participate in volunteer projects overseas at their own expense. These projects last from a few days to several months. The volunteers are retired people, employed people who use vacation time for ministry, or students and other youth who desire an opportunity to serve overseas. This type of involvement has much potential for many Christians. People have more free time today than others have had in the past. And there are many active, retired believers who are financially able to support themselves for periods of service and overseas.

The apostle Paul continues to be the example and the motivation to be a tentmaker overseas. He paid his way through tentmaking in many places where he served. As young men and women hear of modern-day tentmakers, some of them will experience the call of God in their lives to surrender to serve Christ someplace overseas while supporting themselves through a secular vocation.

There are several significant advantages to bivocational foreign missions. Some of them are:

1. Self-employed people can often enter countries which are closed to professional missionaries.
2. Churches can send more missionaries without more financial outlay.
3. Bivocationals meet people in their work daily who need the gospel.
4. Any stigma of the professional missionary is eliminated.
5. The salary and benefits of secular employment are often higher than that of church employment.
6. The salary may be more dependable than support raised from churches and friends at home.
7. A sense of independence may be valuable in being

able to move about or be engaged in various kinds of mission work.

The bivocational foreign missionary need not become the primary approach in foreign missions. But he could become a valid supplement to getting more witnesses out into our world where the gospel is needed. It has worked before.

Responding to the Potential of the Bivocational Staff

One last area of potential facing bivocational ministries today is in the area of the bivocational staff. All kinds of possibilities are open to a church in this area.

Lay members in many churches have held staff positions for many years. Some receive a small salary, and many are unsalaried. The minister of music in one church was the high school choral and band director. The church paid him a small salary to cover any expenses he incurred in this work with the church. Another church had the services of a piano teacher who had abilities in leading a choir. She would not accept any money for her work. Another church had a staff member in the religious education ministry of the church who was a public school music teacher. She, too, was unsalaried in the church. Many of these kinds of people are available to serve as part-time staff members in local churches. They are already trained and can acquire further training in their church responsibilities over the years. They make effective staff members.

In some communities, professionally trained, ordained ministers are available to serve on church staffs in part-time positions. Some of these ministers are retired. They have time, health, and desire to continue in ministry. Churches can employ them as staff members on a part-time basis. Churches are using such retirees as hospital visitors, outreach leaders, and assistant pastors. One retired minister, who was also formerly a denominational leader, was asked to direct senior citizen activities in a church upon his retirement. Financial help in his housing was given him by the church. Another retired pastor was asked to teach some

Bible classes during the week in his church. Another retired minister, who was an ordained minister of music, was asked to serve in a local church as their part-time minister of music. This kind of staff position enables many retired people to continue working on a reduced schedule. It also allows a church to have trained, experienced leadership.

In other communities and cities, trained, ordained ministers are employed in a secular job who also desire to serve in a church ministry. These men are also available for staff positions for a limited number of hours of ministry per week. These ministers may be young or old, but they do not want a full-time churches. They are available for bivocational staff positions.

In other communities, ministers are available from a nearby denominational college or seminary. Often these ministers are permitted to serve local churches in a twenty hour-a-week ministry.

Many reasons for the success of a bivocational staff have been given. One reason often given is financial. A church can accomplish the same thing but utilize more staff leadership with the same money by taking the bivocational route. Another reason given is a sense that, though the concept is new to them, they feel comfortable that it is the Lord's will for them at that time in their church life.

A third explanation for the success of a bivocational staff is the fact that each staff person's gifts and expertise are emphasized. A full-time pastor might be expected to know everything and to do everything needed around the church. In bivocationalism, each staff member contributes his own expertise primarily. Together, they make up a team that meets the needs of the church.

The Clark Street Baptist Church of Johnson City, Tennessee, mentioned earlier, has a bivocational staff of four members. When asked about the advantages of bivocationalism, to them, the staff offered several answers.[13]

1. A sense of independence in not depending primarily upon the church for financial support. The preachers

felt they were freer to preach more prophetically because of this independence.
2. More involvement in the work of the church by the
   membership. The staff could only give leadership, not
   do the work also.
3. Less financial pressure upon the church.
4. Greater awareness of staff job descriptions. Due to
   limited time, each staff position was spelled out specifically. This particular staff met each Wednesday
   night before midweek services for their staff meetings.

Bivocationalism faces great opportunities today. It can
help small churches grow more toward their potential. It can
be the means of starting many new churches. Foreign missions can also use the dual-role minister to preach the gospel
abroad. And local churches can have the benefit of more
staff members for specialized leadership. Its potential might
just be dawning upon our churches, our ministers, and our
denominations.

Notes

1. James L. Lowery, Jr., *Peers, Tents, and Owls* (New York:
Morehouse-Barlow Co., 1973), p. 96.

2. J. T. Burdine, Jr., "Adventure in Ministry: Bivocational Pastorates," *Church Administration* (January 1980): 39.

3. Phillip E. Rodgerson, "The Future of the Small Church in
Non-Metropolitan Areas." An unpublished paper, p. 1.

4. Daryl Heath, "Small Church Effectiveness," *The Quarterly
Review* (October-November-December 1984): 8-12.

5. Elaine Furlow, "Ministers of the Marketplace." A brochure
available from the Church Extension Division of the SBC Home
Mission Board, Atlanta, Ga.

6. Ibid.

7. Robert Hall Glover, *The Progress of World-Wide Missions*,
revised and enlarged by J. Herbert Kane (New York: Harper &
Row, Publishers, 1960), p. 69.

8. J. Christy Wilson, Jr., *Today's Tentmakers* (Wheaton, Ill.: Tyndale House Publishers, 1981), p. 32.

9. Ibid., p. 10.

10. Ibid., pp. 26-37.

11. Ibid., p. 30.

12. See *Annual of the Southern Baptist Convention 1984,* distributed by the SBC Executive Committee, Nashville, Tenn., p. 100.

13. Linda S. Barr, "A Bivocational Team that Really Works," *Church Administration* (April 1984): 21.

Appendix

Church Desiring a Bivocational Pastor
Information Form

Church Name _____ Date _____

Address _____ Phone _____

Association _____

Nearest large town or city _____

Population of your church field _____

1. Describe why you are considering a bi-vocational pastor.

    _____Full-time pastor not practical

    _____Cannot afford a full-time salary

    _____Want a partnership ministry

    _____Other

II. Background information:

  Church membership:

		Sunday School
Active_____	Inactive_____	Enrollment_____

Average
Sunday School Attendance_____

Worship Service
Average Attendance_____

Amount of last pastor's salary and
allowances $_____

Does your church own a parsonage?_____

What is the greatest need in your church?

_____Youth program   _____Outreach

_____Pastoral visitation   _____Needs of the elderly

_____Ministry activities   _____Other

How long was your last pastor there? (Dates)

From_____ to_____

How many years have you had full-time pastors? _____

Has your church ever had a bivocational minister?

_____Yes   _____No   How long?_____

III. Is the congregation willing to take on the responsibilities of a partnership ministry?

_____Yes   _____Probably   _____Don't know

Would your church need help in developing leadership to take over more of the work such as visitation, teaching, managing church facilities, etc.?

_____Yes   _____No

Is such help available through your association? _____

IV. If you were to have a bivocational pastor in your church:

What advantages do you see?

What problems do you anticipate?

What activities do your lay people handle now?

V. What are the most important functions you would want your pastor to perform? Rate them in importance. (Assuming number 1 is highest priority).

VI. Try to identify what you want your bivocational pastor to do and what members of your church could do. Estimate the time required per month.

Pastor/Hours Per Week	Duties	Members/Hours Per Week
_____	Evangelistic visitation	_____
_____	Calling on prospective members	_____
_____	Calling on members	_____
_____	Counseling	_____

             Associational and other
_____ denominational meetings   _____
_____ Sunday School teaching   _____
_____ Youth programs   _____
_____ Social activities   _____
_____ Music   _____
_____ Mimeo/phone/typing/clerical   _____
_____ Worshiping planning   _____
_____ Stewardship, leadership training   _____
_____ Weddings   _____
_____ Funerals   _____
_____ Committee meetings   _____
             How many hours do you feel a pastor
               should devote to study and sermon
_____   preparation?   _____

VII. Would your church be in a position to help a bivocational pastor locate employment?

   ___Yes   ___No

VIII. What type jobs could one reasonably expect to find?

   Estimated Salary $_____

IX. Do you know of a specific job opportunity at this time (in the event a bivocational minister is located quickly)?

   ___Yes   ___No

   If yes, give type of work and estimated salary.

X. Can your church assist financially in relocating a pastor?

   ___Yes   ___No How much? $ _____

XI. Can interim salary be provided while seeking employment?

   ___Yes   ___No How Much? _____

XII. Please write a description of your local church and community, briefly outlining the church's history, growth pattern and outreach in the community. Please share any information that you would like a prospective bivocational pastor to know about your church.

Prospective Bivocational Pastor
Information Form

> These are suggestions of the forms—the questions and format.
> Space limitations restricted exact reproduction of the forms.

NAME _____ Date _____

Present Address _____ Phone _____

Birthdate_____

I. Are you now pastor of a church?

    ___Yes   ___No   Length of time there _____
Describe it: size, location, age, etc.

II. Summarize your church experiences: dates of pastorates, etc.

III. Summarize your secular work background.

IV. Describe your skills and degree of proficiency (good, excellent, etc.).

Skill	Proficiency	Training Or Years Experience

V. Summarize your educational background.

School	Years Attended	Degree or Certificate Received

VI. Why does bivocational ministry appeal to you?

What advantages do you see?

What disadvantages?

VII. Family information:
Number of children, sex and age:

General condition of your health:

____Fair   ____Good   ____Excellent
Your wife's health:

____Fair   ____Good   ____Excellent
Any disabilities or handicaps? Describe:

VIII. Describe the financial arrangement, if you currently serve a
church.

$_____Budget $_____Your Salary

$_____Housing $_____Automobile

Is annuity provided?____ Health insurance?____

IX. List some things you would expect of a church your serve as
bivocational minister (training, visitation, teaching, ministry,
etc.).

What salary would you expect?

$_____Church $_____Secular Employment

$_____Total

X. What problems do you anticipate as a bivocational minister?

XI. Assuming you work 40 hours per week at a secular job—how
much time do you think you can give to the following: (hours
per week)

____Ministry and evangelism visitation

____Sermon preparation

____Denominational meetings

_____Your family

_____Reading and study

XII. In what specific area of the U.S. would you like to work?

XIII. What help would you need in locating a secular job?

XIV. What financial help would you need to visit a prospective church?

XV. Would you consider going to an area where there is no Southern Baptist church with the purpose of starting one?

_____Yes   _____No

XVI. Would you be willing to participate in a special orientation relating to your new area of work?

_____Yes   _____No

XVII. Write a paragraph describing how you feel about evangelistic visitation.

XVIII. References: List the names of your director of associational missions and six people who know you reasonably well and are acquainted with your ministry.

XIX. Please share your call to the ministry and why you feel God may be leading you into a bivocational ministry in pioneer missions. Also, give any other information you would like to share with a church.

Covenant for Ministry

PASTOR Hours per week	Ministries	TOTAL Hours per week	MEMBERS Hours per week
____	Evangelistic Visitation	____	____
____	Calling on Prospective members	____	____
____	Calling on members	____	____
____	Calling on the sick	____	____
____	Counseling	____	____
____	Assnl./other denominational meetings	____	____
____	Sunday School teaching	____	____
____	Church Training	____	____
____	Youth programs	____	____
____	Woman's Missionary Union	____	____
____	Social activities	____	____
____	Brotherhood	____	____
____	Music	____	____
____	Mimeo/phone/typing/clerical	____	____
____	Worship planning	____	____
____	Stewardship planning	____	____
____	Leadership training	____	____
____	Weddings	____	____
____	Funerals	____	____
____	Personal crises	____	____
____	Committee meetings	____	____
____	Other (add to this list for local field)	____	____
____	How many hours do you feel your pastor should devote to study and sermon preparation?	____	____

Bibliography

A. Books and Commentaries

Allen, Roland. *Missionary Methods: St. Paul's or Ours.* Grand Rapids: Eerdmans, 1962.

Allen, Roland. *The Spontaneous Expansion of the Church and the Causes Which Hinder It.* Grand Rapids: Eerdmans, 1962.

Armstrong, O. K. and Marjorie. *Baptists Who Shaped a Nation.* Nashville: Baptist Press, 1975.

Barclay, William. *The Daily Study Bible Series, The Acts of the Apostles.* 2nd ed. Philadelphia: The Westminster Press, 1955.

Barclay, William. *The Letters to the Corinthians. The Daily Study Bible Series.* 2nd ed. Philadelphia: The Westminster Press, 1956.

Battenson, Henry, ed. *Documents of the Christian Church.* 2nd ed. London: Oxford University, 1975.

Colson, Mary. *Heroes of the Faith.* Nashville: Baptist Press, 1954.

Cox, Samuel. *An Expositor's Notebook.* Philadelphia: Smith, English, and Co., 1873.

Dudley, Carl S. *Making the Small Church Effective.* Nashville: Abingdon, 1978.

Elliott, John T. *Our Pastor Has an Outside Job.* Valley Forge: Judson Press, 1980.

Eusebius. *Ecclesiastical History.* Translated by Christian Frederick Cruse. New York: Stanford & Swords, 1850.

Exell, Joseph S. *I Corinthians,* vol. 17. *Biblical Illustrator,* 23 vols. Grand Rapids: Baker Book House, n.d.

Glover, Robert Hall. *The Progress of World-Wide Missions.* Revised and enlarged by J. Herbert Kane. New York: Harper & Row Publishers, 1960.

Hastings, James, ed., "Scribes." *Enclyclopedia of Religion and Ethics,* vol. XI. New York: Charles Scribner's Son, 1920.

Hoadley, Frank T. and Benjamin Browne. *Baptists Who Dared.* Valley Forge: Judson Press, 1980.

Horn, Clifford. *A Tent-Making Ministry.* Tokoyo: Concordia-Sah, Japan Lutheran Church, 1971.

Lenski, R. C. H. *Interpretation of First & Second Peter, First, Second & Third Peter, John, Jude,* Vol. 11. Minneapolis, Minn.: Augsburg Publishing House, 1966.

Lowery, James L., Jr., ed. *Case Histories of Tentmakers.* Wilton, Conn.: Morehouse-Barlow Co., 1973.

Lowery, James L., Jr. *More Case Histories.* Boston: Enablement Inc., 1978.

Lowery, James L., Jr. *Peers, Tents, and Owls.* New York: Morehouse-Barlow Co., 1973.

Miller, Marvin J. *The Case for a Tentmaking Ministry.* Elkhart, Indiana: Mennonite Board of Missions, 1978.

Marshall, I. Howard. *The Acts of the Apostles,* vol. 5. The Tyndale New Testament Commentaries. 20 vols. R.V.G. Tasker. Grand Rapids: Wm. B. Eerdmans Publishing Company, 1981.

Orr, James, ed., "Scribes." *International Standard Bible Encllyclopedia,* vol. IV. Grand Rapids: Wm. B. Eerdmans Publishers, 1960.

Robertson, A. T. *The Acts of the Apostles,* vol. 3. Word Pictures in the New Testament. Nashville: Broadman Press, 1930.

Schaller, Lyle E. *The Small Church IS Different.* Nashville: Abingdon Press, 1982.

Smith, T. C. and Dale Moody. *Acts-I Corinthians,* vol. 10. The Broadman Bible Commentary. 12 vols. Clifton J. Allen, gen. ed. Nashville: Broadman Press, 1970.

Starkes, M. Thomas. *Toward a Theology of Missions.* AMG Publishers: Aurora, Ontario, 1984.

Tasker, R. V. G., *The Acts of the Apostles,* vol. 5 The Tyndale New Testament Commentaries. Grand Rapids: Wm. B. Eerdmans Publishing Company, 1981. 5. *The Acts of the Apostles.* By I. Howard Marshall.

Tenney, Merrill C., ed. "Hosea." *The Zondervan Pictorial Bible Dictionary.* 3d ed. Grand Rapids: Zondervan Publishing House, 1964.

Vogt, Virgil. *The Christian Calling.* Scottdale, Penn.: Herald Press, 1961.

Wilson, J. Christy, Jr. *Today's Tentmakers.* Wheaton, Ill.: Tyndale House, 1981.

Yoder, John Howard. *As You Go: The Old Mission in a New Day.* Scottdale, Penn.: Herald Press, 1961.

B. Periodicals and Journals

Allred, Hoyle T. "The Bivocational Pastor and the Baptist Association." *Church Administration* (December 1981): 47. "The Director of Missions and the Bivocational Pastor." *Church Administration* (February 1981): 41-42. "Priorities for Keeping a Church." *Church Administration* (September 1982): 33-34.

Allred, Thurman W. "A Bivocational Church Staff?" *Church Administration* (January 1981): 33-34.

_____. "Bi-Vocational: A Rich Heritage." *Church Administration* (November 1980): 39-40.

_____. "Called and Committed." *Church Administration* (October 1980): 37-38.

_____. "Hey! Counselor." *Church Administration* (March 1982): 38-39.

Barr, Linda S. "A Bivocational Team That Really Works." *Church Administration* (April 1984): 20-21.

Bartlett, Allen, Jr. "Part Time Clergy." *The Tentmaker's Journal.* (January-February 1981): 2.

Brewer, Paul. "We Are Southern Baptists: How We Grew Through Revivals." *Church Training* (July 1982): 19-21.

Burdine, J. T., Jr. "Adventure in Ministry Bivocational Pastorates." *Church Administration* (January 1980): 39-40.

_____. "The Bivocational Call." *The Tentmaker's Journal.* (March-April 1980): 4.

_____. "The Bivocational Minister as Administrator." *Church Administration* (June 1981): 43-44.

_____. "Covenant for Ministry." *The Tentmaker's Journal.* (March-April 1981): 4, 6.

_____. "Covenant for Ministry." *The Tentmaker's Journal.* (May-June 1980): 5-6.

_____. "The Number of Bivocational Pastors." *Church Administration* (April 1982): 41-42.

————. "One Ministry." *The Tentmaker's Journal.* (November-December 1980): 4.

————. "One Ministry: Information Resources for the Bivocational Pastor." *The Tentmaker's Journal.* (July-August 1980): 4.

————. "One Ministry: Long Range Planning for Growth." *The Tentmaker's Journal.* (September-October 1980): 4.

Cantrell, Glen. "Are There Differences in Bi-vocational 'Pastors' and 'Preachers'?" *The Tentmaker's Journal.* (September-October 1980): 3.

Carter, James E. "The Socioeconomic Status of Baptist Ministers in Historical Perspective." *Baptist History and Heritage* XV (January 1980): 37-44.

Carter, Ken. "The Evangelistic Responsibility of the Bivocational Pastor." *Associational Administration Bulletin* (March-April 1979): 5.

Chadwick, Marilynn. "Profiles in Ministry: Paul DeArmas." *The Tentmaker's Journal* (January-February 1981): 6, 11.

Chandler, John R. "The Pastor and Part-Time Music Director Working Together." *Church Administration* (February 1981): 7-9.

Cooper, Ray, ed. "Profiles in Ministry: Can Preaching and Paint Mix?" *The Tentmaker's Journal* (March-April 1980): 7.

————. "Profiles in Ministry: Co-Laborers in Christ." *The Tentmaker's Journal* (May-June 1980): 7.

————. "Profiles in Ministry: First Things First." *The Tentmaker's Journal* (March-April 1980): 7.

————. "Profiles in Ministry: God's Cultivator." *The Tentmaker's Journal* (May-June 1980): 7.

————. "Profiles in Ministry: Reverend Louis A. Newby." *The Tentmaker's Journal* (September-October 1980): 6.

————. "Profiles in Ministry: Tentmakers Organize Services for the 810th." *The Tentmaker's Journal* (July-August 1980): 6.

————. "Tanner Speaks His Mind on Bi-vocational Ministers." *The Tentmaker's Journal* (Fall 1981): 3.

Dale, Robert D. "Hidden Advantages of Tentmakers." *The Tentmaker's Journal.* (March-April 1980): 4.

Davis, C. P. "Delegate Tasks and Develop the Church." *Church Administration* (December 1981): 22-24.

Dennis, Nodell, "The Bivocational Pastor and Self-Esteem." *Church Administration* (June 1982):43-44.

Dykes, Davis O., "Full-time Staff Meetings with a Part-time Staff."
    Church Administration (February 1981): 15-16.

Elliott, John Y., "Dual-Role Clergy." *Christian Ministry.* (Septem-
    ber 1978): 27-28.

Farley, Gary. "The Bivocational Minister." *Search* (Summer 1977):
    51-63.

Fisher, Desmond. "Worker-Priests Once More." *Frontier* 10 (Sum-
    mer 1967): 140.

Greenwood, Dorothy, and Lipsett, Lawrence. "Tentmaking: Mod-
    ern Style." *Christian Ministry.* (September 1981): 26-28.

Grubb, Anne. "English Worker Priests." *Frontier* 3 (Winter 1960):
    267ff.

Hancock, Charles. "The Place of Bivocationalism." *Church Ad-
    ministration* (June 1983): 17-18.

Hayes, David W. "Work More Effectively with Your Part-time
    Minister of Education and Youth." *Church Administration*
    (February 1981): 13-14.

Hayes, Judi Slayden. "An Interview with a Bivocational Staff."
    Search (Spring 1984): 45-50.

Head, K. Maynard. "Deacons Can Become Co-Ministers with Bi-
    Vocational Pastors." *The Tentmaker's Journal.* (March-April
    1981): 2.

_____. "Housing Options for the Bivocational Pastor." *Church
    Administration* (February 1982): 43-44.

_____. "Involving Laypersons in Ministry." *Church Administra-
    tion* (November 1981): 42-43.

_____. "Pastoral Visitation and the Bivocational Minister."
    Church Administration (March 1981): 43-44.

_____. "The Bivocational Pastor and Stress." *Church Adminis-
    tration* (June 1983): 18-20.

_____. "The Bivocational Pastor & Time." *The Tentmaker's Jour-
    nal.* (November-December 1980): 9.

_____. "The Bivocational Pastor and the Association." *Church
    Administration* (December 1980): 41.42.

_____. "The Bivocational Pastor: Linking Church and Pastor in
    a Rewarding Relationship." *Church Administration* (April
    1981): 44-45.

Heath, Daryl. "Small Church Effectiveness." *The Quarterly Re-
    view* 45 (October-December 1984): 8-12.

Helmich, Robert C. "Bivocational—Not Second Class . . . ." *Church Administration* (August 1982): 45-46.

Hill, L. Donald. "The Bivocational Pastor and Family Relationships." *Church Administration* (July 1981):39-40.

Holloway, Dale. "Frustrations and Joys of a Bi-vocational Pastor." *The Lifelong Learner* (February 1979): 1-2.

Lamb, Robert. "Bivocational Pastors Upset Treasured Assumptions." *The Tentmaker's Journal* (March-April 1980): 5.

Liechti, Steve, et al. "A Look at Worker-Priest Ministry by Some People Who Are in It." *Currents in Theology and Missions* (February 1982): 41-46.

Lowry, Jim. "Forced Terminations: Dilemma Embarrasses SBC," *Facts & Trends* (February 1984): 10, 15.

————. "Reaching People Effort Launched." *Facts & Trends* (February 1982): 4.

————. "Study Lists Salaries, Benefits." *Facts & Trends* (October 1982): 12.

McCarty, Doran. "The Bi-vocational Minister and His Ministry." *Associational Administration Bulletin* (March-April 1979): 1-4.

Nelson, James. "A Support System for the Bi-vocational Pastor: Interview with James Nelson." *Associational Administration Bulletin* (March-April 1979): 10-11.

Nelson, James. "Being Supportive to the Bi-vocational Pastor." *Associational Administration Bulletin* (April-May 1977): 6.

Nelson, James. "How Shall They Lead?" *The Lifelong Learner* (October 1979): 1.

Nelson, James. "New Needs—Met by Old Methods." *Associational Administration Bulletin* (March-April 1979): 5.

Nelson, James. "The Call to Bi-vocational Ministry." *The Lifelong Learner* (August 1978): 102.

Oates, Wayne. "Tentmakers Testimony: My Life and the Bi-Vocational Ministry." *The Tentmaker's Journal* (May-June 1980): 3.

Parker, Teresa Sheilds. "Preaching, Farming Go Hand-in-Hand." *The Tentmaker's Journal* (November-December 1980): 6, 11.

Phol, Direktor A. "The Service of the Pastor in a World Come of Age." *Foundations* (April-June 1975): 102-106.

Porter, Thomas W. "Pastor-Workers and Minister-Workers." *Christian Century,* 16 February 1972, pp. 198-200.

Prather, Tom T. "What Hat Today?" *The Tentmaker's Journal* (December 1981): 4.

Price, W. Wayne "Redeeming the Time." *The Tentmaker's Journal* (September-October 1980): 7.

Redding, George W., "Paul: Staking His Ministry in Tent-Making." *The Tentmaker's Journal* 1, no. 3 (July-August 1980): 3.

Shabag, Wayne. "Into All the World." *The Tentmaker's Journal* (November-December 1980): 5, 11.

Sharp, Charles E., "The Pastor and the Part-Time Staff." *Church Administration* (March 1980): 37-39.

Simmons, D. Glenn. "The Deacon and the Bivocational Pastor." *The Deacon* (January-March 1983): 39-40.

Smith, Gean D. "A Two-Hatted Pastor." *The Tentmaker's Journal* (March-April 1981): 6.

Stanton, Jim. "A Part-time Minister of Recreation May Be Your Answer." *Church Administration* (February 1981): 11-12.

Touchton, Judy. "The Bi-vocational Pastor." *Home Missions* (October 1977): 4-17.

Williams, Melvin G. "Hire a Tent-Maker". *Christian Ministry* (January 1981): 19-20.

Willis, Charles. "Bivocational Pastors: Denominational Role Is Vital." *Facts & Trends* (Mary 1983): 1, 12.

Wingo, Lewis. "The Needs of Bi-Vocational Pastors." *The Quarterly Review* (April-June 1979): 41-55.

Wyatt, Neal. "The Bivocational Pastor: His Contributions and Unique Relationship to Churches." *Church Administration* (June 1983): 20-21.

C. General Materials

Annual of the Southern Baptist Convention 1984. Distributed by the SBC Executive Committee, Nashville, Tenn.

Burdine, J. T., Jr. "Alabama Bivocational Pastors Survey Summary." A report from Rural Urban Department of the Home Mission Board, SBC, Atlanta, Ga., 1980.

_____. "Bivocational Pastors of Southern Baptist Churches." A report from Rural Urban Department of the Home Mission Board, SBC, Atlanta, Ga., 1981.

Burham, John C. "Equipping Bivocational Pastors in St. Joseph Baptist Association." D.Min. project, Midwestern Baptist Theological Seminary, 1982.

Clergy Occupational Development and Employment Project. *Dual-*

Role Pastorates. Rochester: Clergy Occupational Development and Employment Project, 1978.

Dennis, Robert Nodell. "Building Self-Image in Bi-vocational Pastors." D.Min. project, Southwestern Baptist Theological Seminary, 1981.

Furlow, Elaine. "Ministers of the Marketplace." A brochure from Church Extension Division, Home Mission Board, SBC, n.d.

Grimes, Clyde L. "Establishment of an Institute for Bi-vocational Church Leaders in Collin County, Texas." D. Min. project, Southwestern Baptist Theological Seminary, 1982.

Hinton, Leonard O. "Bi-Vocational Pastors." A report from Research Division of the Home Mission Board, SBC, Atlanta, Ga., 1980.

Holloway, Dale. "Ministers of the Marketplace." A brochure published by Rural-Urban Missions Department, Home Mission Board, SBC, Atlanta, Ga., 1982.

Reko, H. Karl. "Determinative Factors in the Ability of Christ Seminary—Seminex Graduates to Conduct Worker-Priest Ministries in the United States." D.Min. thesis, Eden Theological Seminary, 1980.

Rodgerson, Phillip E. "The Future of the Small Church in Non-Metropolitan Areas." A paper from the Virginia Baptist General Board, Richmond, Virginia.

Rogers, Ernie Don. "A Seminar on Biblical Preaching for the Bivocational Pastor." D.Min. project, Southwestern Baptist Theological Seminary, 1981.

"Southern Baptist Tentmaker Tracks." A newsletter published by the Home Mission Board SBC, Atlanta, Ga., July 24, 1956.

Washington, Jack L. "Study of Bivocational Pastors and Churches in the Southern Baptist Convention, 1983." A report from Program Research Department, Home Mission Board, SBC, Atlanta, Ga., 1984.

D.   Video Tapes

"Bivocational Ministries: The Struggles for Acceptance," Part 1. Produced by the Home Mission Board, SBC, Atlanta, Ga.

"Bivocational Ministries: The Struggles for Acceptance," Part 2. Produced by the Home Mission Board, SBC, Atlanta, Ga.

"Bivocational Ministries: Whatever It Takes." Produced by the Home Mission Board, SBC, Atlanta, Ga.